Glencoe McGraw-Hill

Math Connects
Course 1

Chapter 6
Resource Masters

McGraw Hill Glencoe

Consumable Workbooks Many of the worksheets contained in the Chapter Resource
Masters are available as consumable workbooks in both English and Spanish.

	MHID	ISBN
Study Guide and Intervention Workbook	0-07-881032-9	978-0-07-881032-9
Skills Practice Workbook	0-07-881031-0	978-0-07-881031-2
Practice Workbook	0-07-881034-5	978-0-07-881034-3
Word Problem Practice Workbook	0-07-881033-7	978-0-07-881033-6

Spanish Versions

Study Guide and Intervention Workbook	0-07-881036-1	978-0-07-881036-7
Skills Practice Workbook	0-07-881035-3	978-0-07-881035-0
Practice Workbook	0-07-881038-8	978-0-07-881038-1
Word Problem Practice Workbook	0-07-881037-X	978-0-07-881037-4

Answers for Workbooks The answers for Chapter 6 of these workbooks can be found in the
back of this Chapter Resource Masters booklet.

StudentWorks Plus™ This CD-ROM includes the entire Student Edition test along with the
English workbooks listed above.

TeacherWorks Plus™ All of the materials found in this booklet are included for viewing,
printing, and editing in this CD-ROM.

Spanish Assessment Masters (MHID: 0-07-881039-6, ISBN: 978-0-07-881039-8)
These masters contain a Spanish version of Chapter 6 Test Form 2A and Form 2C.

 **Glencoe**

The McGraw-Hill Companies

Send all inquiries to:
Glencoe/McGraw-Hill
8787 Orion Place
Columbus, OH 43240

ISBN: 978-0-07-881024-4
MHID: 0-07-881024-8

Math Connects, Course 1

Printed in the United States of America.
4 5 6 7 8 9 10 REL 16 15 14 13 12 11 10

CONTENTS

Teacher's Guide to Using the
Chapter 6 Resource Masters

The *Chapter 6 Resource Masters* includes the core materials needed for Chapter 6. These materials include worksheets, extensions, and assessment options. The answers for these pages appear at the back of this booklet.

All of the materials found in this booklet are included for viewing and printing on the *TeacherWorks Plus*™ CD-ROM.

Chapter Resources

Student-Built Glossary (pages 1–2) These masters are a student study tool that presents up to twenty of the key vocabulary terms from the chapter. Students are to record definitions and/or examples for each term. You may suggest that students highlight or star the terms with which they are not familiar. Give this to students before beginning Lesson 6-1. Encourage them to add these pages to their mathematics study notebooks. Remind them to complete the appropriate words as they study each lesson.

Family Letter and Family Activity (pages 3–6) The letter informs your students' families of the mathematics they will be learning in this chapter. The family activity helps them to practice problems that are similar to those on the state test. A full solution for each problem is included. Spanish versions of these pages are also included. Give these to students to take home before beginning the chapter.

Anticipation Guide (pages 7–8) This master, presented in both English and Spanish, is a survey used before beginning the chapter to pinpoint what students may or may not know about the concepts in the chapter. Students will revisit this survey after they complete the chapter to see if their perceptions have changed.

Lesson Resources

Lesson Reading Guide Get Ready for the Lesson reiterates the questions from the beginning of the Student Edition lesson. Read the Lesson asks students to interpret the context of and relationships among terms in the lesson. Finally, Remember What You Learned asks students to summarize what they have learned using various representation techniques. Use as a study tool for note taking or as an informal reading assignment. It is also a helpful tool for ELL (English Language Learners).

Study Guide and Intervention This master provides vocabulary, key concepts, additional worked-out examples and Check Your Progress exercises to use as a reteaching activity. It can also be used in conjunction with the Student Edition as an instructional tool for students who have been absent.

Skills Practice This master focuses more on the computational nature of the lesson. Use as an additional practice option or as homework for second-day teaching of the lesson.

Practice This master closely follows the types of problems found in the Exercises section of the Student Edition and includes word problems. Use as an additional practice option or as homework for second-day teaching of the lesson.

Word Problem Practice This master includes additional practice in solving word problems that apply the concepts of the lesson. Use as an additional practice or as homework for second-day teaching of the lesson.

Enrichment These activities may extend the concepts of the lesson, offer a historical or multicultural look at the concepts, or widen students' perspectives on the mathematics they are learning. They are written for use with all levels of students.

Graphing Calculator, Scientific Calculator, or Spreadsheet Activities These activities present ways in which technology can be used with the concepts in some lessons of this chapter. Use as an alternative approach to some concepts or as an integral part of your lesson presentation.

Assessment Options

The assessment masters in the *Chapter 6 Resource Masters* offer a wide range of assessment tools for formative (monitoring) assessment and summative (final) assessment.

Student Recording Sheet This master corresponds with the Test Practice at the end of the chapter.

Extended-Response Rubric This master provides information for teachers and students on how to assess performance on open-ended questions.

Quizzes Four free-response quizzes offer assessment at appropriate intervals in the chapter.

Mid-Chapter Test This 1-page test provides an option to assess the first half of the chapter. It parallels the timing of the Mid-Chapter Quiz in the Student Edition and includes both multiple-choice and free-response questions.

Vocabulary Test This test is suitable for all students. It includes a list of vocabulary words and 10 questions to assess students' knowledge of those words. This can also be used in conjunction with one of the leveled chapter tests.

Leveled Chapter Tests

- *Form 1* contains multiple-choice questions and is intended for use with below grade level students.

- *Forms 2A and 2B* contain multiple-choice questions aimed at on grade level students. These tests are similar in format to offer comparable testing situations.

- *Forms 2C and 2D* contain free-response questions aimed at on grade level students. These tests are similar in format to offer comparable testing situations.

- *Form 3* is a free-response test for use with above grade level students.

All of the above mentioned tests include a free-response Bonus question.

Extended-Response Test Performance assessment tasks are suitable for all students. Samples answers and a scoring rubric are included for evaluation.

Standardized Test Practice These three pages are cumulative in nature. It includes two parts: multiple-choice questions with bubble-in answer format and short-answer free-response questions.

Answers

- The answers for the Anticipation Guide and Lesson Resources are provided as reduced pages with answers appearing in red.

- Full-size answer keys are provided for the assessment masters.

Student-Built Glossary

This is an alphabetical list of new vocabulary terms you will learn in Chapter 6. As you study the chapter, complete each term's definition or description. Remember to add the page number where you found the term. Add this page to your math study notebook to review vocabulary at the end of the chapter.

Vocabulary Term	Found on Page	Definition/Description/Example
arithmetic sequence		
equivalent ratio		
proportion		
proportional		
rate		
ratio		

6 Student-Built Glossary *(continued)*

Vocabulary Term	Found on Page	Definition/Description/Example
ratio table		
scaling		
sequence		
term		
unit rate		

6 **Family Letter**

Dear Parent or Guardian:

Ratios, rates, and proportions help us to make decisions. We can use them to make models of objects and to determine distances on a map. We can also use them to make budget decisions, to determine the better buy at a grocery store, and to calculate sales tax.

In Chapter 6, Ratio, Proportion, and Functions, your child will learn how to express ratios and rates, how to use ratio tables, what proportions are and how to solve them, about sequences and expressions, and about using proportions in equations. Your child will complete a variety of daily classroom assignments and activities and possibly produce a chapter project.

By signing this letter and returning it with your child, you agree to encourage your child by getting involved. Enclosed is an activity you can do with your child that practices how the math we will be learning in Chapter 6 might be tested. You may also wish to log on to **glencoe.com** for self-check quizzes and other study help. If you have any questions or comments, feel free to contact me at school.

Sincerely,

Signature of Parent or Guardian _____ Date _____

6 Family Activity

State Test Practice

Fold the page along the dashed line. Work each problem on another piece of paper. Then unfold the page to check your work.

1.

What is the ratio of stars to balloons?

A 3 : 4

B 4 : 7

C 4 : 3

D 7 : 4

2. Kara is practicing her free throw shot. She is averaging 7 shots made out of every 11 attempted. How many shots would you expect her to make if she attempted 55?

A 21

B 35

C 51

D 42

Fold here.

Solution

1. *Hint: Ratios are listed in the specified order, for example the ratio of A to B is A:B, not B:A.*

There are 4 stars and 3 balloons. The problem asks for the ratio of stars to balloons, so the number of stars will be first in the ratio, or 4 : 3.

Solution

2. *Hint: She is attempting 5 times as many shots as the total in the provided ratio.*

If she attempted 55 shots, it would be 5 times as many as 11, and since we expect her to make 7 out of 11, we can expect her to make 7 × 5, or 35 out of 55.

You can also use a ratio.

$$\frac{7}{11} = \frac{?}{55}$$

The denominator is multiplied by 5, so the same will be true of the numerator.

The answer is **C**.

The answer is **B**.

6 Carta a la familia

Estimado padre o apoderado:

Las razones, las tasas y las proporciones nos ayudan a tomar decisiones. Las usamos para hacer modelos de objetos y determinar las distancias en un mapa. También nos sirven para tomar decisiones de presupuestos, para determinar cuáles son las mejores compras en el supermercado y calcular el impuesto sobre las ventas.

En el **Capítulo 6, Razones, proporciones y funciones**, su hijo(a) aprenderá a expresar razones y tasas, a usar tablas de razones, saber qué son las proporciones y cómo resolverlas, aprender sobre sucesiones y expresiones; y sobre el uso de proporciones en ecuaciones. En el estudio de este capítulo, su hijo(a) completará una variedad de tareas y actividades diarias y es posible que trabaje en un proyecto del capítulo.

Al firmar esta carta y devolverla con su hijo(a), usted se compromete a ayudarlo(a) a participar en su aprendizaje. Junto con esta carta, va incluida una actividad que puede realizar con él(ella) y la cual practica lo que podrían encontrar en las pruebas de los conceptos matemáticos que aprenderán en el Capítulo 6. Además, visiten **glencoe.com** para ver autocontroles y otras ayudas para el estudio. Si tiene cualquier pregunta o comentario, por favor contácteme en la escuela.

Cordialmente,

Firma del padre o apoderado _____ Fecha _____

6 Actividad en familia

Práctica para la prueba estatal

Doblen la página a lo largo de las líneas punteadas. Resuelvan cada problema en otra hoja de papel. Luego, desdoblen la página y revisen las respuestas.

1.

¿Cuál es la razón de estrellas a globos?

   A 3 : 4
   B 4 : 7
   C 4 : 3
   D 7 : 4

2. Kara practica un tiro libre. Convierte un promedio de 7 tiros por cada 11 que intenta. ¿Cuántos tiros se espera que convierta si intenta 55?

   A 21
   B 35
   C 51
   D 42

Doblen aquí.

Solución

1. *Ayuda: Las razones se enumeran en un orden específico; por ejemplo, la razón de A a B es A:B, no B:A.*

   Hay 4 estrellas y 3 globos. El problema pide la razón de estrellas a globos; entonces, el número de estrellas irá primero en la razón ó 4:3.

Solución

2. *Ayuda: Ella intenta convertir 5 tiros más que el total de la razón dada.*

   Si intenta convertir 55 tiros, sería 5 veces más que 11; y como esperamos que logre 7 de 11, esperamos que convierta 7×5 ó 35 de 55.

   También pueden usar una razón.

   $$\frac{7}{11} = \frac{?}{55}$$

   El denominador se multiplica por 5; por lo tanto, lo mismo se aplica al numerador.

La respuesta es **C**. | La respuesta es **B**.

6 Anticipation Guide

Ratio, Proportion, and Functions

STEP 1 *Before you begin Chapter 6*

- Read each statement.
- Decide whether you Agree (A) or Disagree (D) with the statement.
- Write A or D in the first column OR if you are not sure whether you agree or disagree, write NS (Not Sure).

STEP 1 A, D, or NS	Statement	STEP 2 A or D
	1. A ratio is a comparison of two numbers by division.	
	2. A ratio can be simplified in the same way as a fraction.	
	3. A rate is a ratio of two measurements with the same kind of units.	
	4. An example of a unit rate is $\frac{132 \text{ miles}}{2 \text{ hours}}$.	
	5. $\frac{3}{5} = \frac{12}{20}$ is an example of a proportion.	
	6. Cross products can be used to determine if two ratios form a proportion.	
	7. Looking for patterns in a problem can lead to a solution.	
	8. A sequence is a list of numbers in order from least to greatest.	
	9. Each number in a sequence is called a factor of that sequence.	
	10. The equation $y = 5x$ could represent a sequence in which each output is equal to 5 times the input.	

STEP 2 *After you complete Chapter 6*

- Reread each statement and complete the last column by entering an A (Agree) or a D (Disagree).
- Did any of your opinions about the statements change from the first column?
- For those statements that you mark with a D, use a separate sheet of paper to explain why you disagree. Use examples, if possible.

6 Ejercicios preparatorios

Razones, proporciones y funciones

PASO 1   *Antes de comenzar el Capítulo 6*

- Lee cada enunciado.

- Decide si estás de acuerdo (A) o en desacuerdo (D) con el enunciado.

- Escribe A o D en la primera columna O si no estás seguro(a) de la respuesta, escribe NS (No estoy seguro(a)).

PASO 1 A, D o NS	Enunciado	PASO 2 A o D
	1. Una razón es una comparación de dos números mediante división.	
	2. Una razón puede reducirse de la misma manera que una fracción.	
	3. Una tasa es una razón de dos mediciones con el mismo tipo de unidades.	
	4. Un ejemplo de tasa unitaria es $\frac{132 \text{ millas}}{2 \text{ horas}}$.	
	5. $\frac{3}{5} = \frac{12}{20}$ es un ejemplo de proporción.	
	6. Los productos cruzados pueden utilizarse para determinar si dos razones forman una proporción.	
	7. Buscar patrones en un problema puede conducir a una solución.	
	8. Una sucesión es una lista de números ordenados del más pequeño al más grande.	
	9. Cada número en una sucesión se denomina factor de la sucesión.	
	10. La ecuación $y = 5x$ puede representar una sucesión en la cual cada valor de salida es igual a 5 veces el valor de entrada.	

PASO 2   *Después de completar el Capítulo 6*

- Vuelve a leer cada enunciado y completa la última columna con una A o una D.

- ¿Cambió cualquiera de tus opiniones sobre los enunciados de la primera columna?

- En una hoja de papel aparte, escribe un ejemplo de por qué estás en desacuerdo con los enunciados que marcaste con una D.

6-1 Lesson Reading Guide

Ratios and Rates

Get Ready for the Lesson

Complete the Mini Lab at the top of page 314 in your textbook. Write your answers below.

1. Compare the number of blue paper clips to the number of red paper clips using the word *more* and then using the word *times*.

2. Compare the number of red paper clips to the number of blue paper clips using the word *less* and then using a fraction.

Read the Lesson

3. A ratio compares amounts of two different things by division. Tell what different things are compared in the examples in your textbook.

   Example 1 _____

   Example 2 _____

4. Write the ratio of *2 pens out of a total of 3 pens* 3 different ways.

   _____   _____   _____

5. What is the denominator in a unit rate?

Remember What You Learned

6. Go to your local grocery store and make a list of unit rates that are used to price items in the store. Also, compare prices for different brands of a certain product. How can you find out which brand provides the best value? Does the store help you to make the comparison? If so, how?

6-1 Study Guide and Intervention

Ratios and Rates

A **ratio** is a comparison of two numbers by division. A common way to express a ratio is as a fraction in simplest form. Ratios can also be written in other ways. For example, the ratio $\frac{2}{3}$ can be written as 2 to 3, 2 out of 3, or 2:3.

Examples   Refer to the diagram at the right.

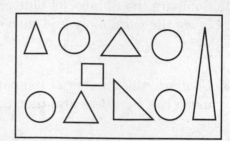

1 Write the ratio in simplest form that compares the number of circles to the number of triangles.

circles → $\frac{4}{5}$ The GCF of 4 and 5 is 1.
triangles →

So, the ratio of circles to triangles is $\frac{4}{5}$, 4 to 5, or 4:5.
For every 4 circles, there are 5 triangles.

2 Write the ratio in simplest form that compares the number of circles to the total number of figures.

circles → $\frac{4}{10} = \frac{2}{5}$ The GCF of 4 and 10 is 2.
total figures →

The ratio of circles to the total number of figures is $\frac{2}{5}$, 2 to 5, or 2:5.
For every two circles, there are five total figures.

A **rate** is a ratio of two measurements having different kinds of units. When a rate is simplified so that it has a denominator of 1, it is called a **unit rate**.

Example 3   Write the ratio *20 students to 5 computers* as a unit rate.

$$\frac{20 \text{ students}}{5 \text{ computers}} = \frac{4 \text{ students}}{1 \text{ computer}}$$ Divide the numerator and the denominator by 5 to get a denominator of 1.

The ratio written as a unit rate is *4 students to 1 computer*.

Exercises

Write each ratio as a fraction in simplest form.

1. 2 guppies out of 6 fish

2. 12 puppies to 15 kittens

3. 5 boys out of 10 students

Write each rate as a unit rate.

4. 6 eggs for 3 people

5. $12 for 4 pounds

6. 40 pages in 8 days

6-1 Skills Practice

Ratios and Rates

Write each ratio as a fraction in simplest form.

1. 3 sailboats to 6 motorboats

2. 4 tulips to 9 daffodils

3. 5 baseballs to 25 softballs

4. 2 days out of 8 days

5. 6 poodles out of 18 dogs

6. 10 yellow eggs out of 12 colored eggs

7. 12 sheets of paper out of 28

8. 18 hours out of 24 hours

9. 16 elms out of 20 trees

10. 15 trumpets to 9 trombones

11. 5 ducks to 30 geese

12. 14 lions to 10 tigers

13. 6 sodas out of 16 drinks

14. 20 blue jays out of 35 birds

Write each rate as a unit rate.

15. 14 hours in 2 weeks

16. 36 pieces of candy for 6 children

17. 8 teaspoons for 4 cups

18. 8 tomatoes for $2

19. $28 for 4 hours

20. 150 miles in 3 hours

21. $18 for 3 CDs

22. 48 logs on 6 trucks

23. Write the ratio *21 wins to 9 losses* as a fraction in simplest form.

24. Write the ratio *$12 dollars for 3 tickets* as a unit rate.

Lesson 6–1

6-1 Practice

Ratios and Rates

1. **FRUITS** Find the ratio of bananas to oranges in the graphic at the right. Write the ratio as a fraction in simplest form. Then explain its meaning.

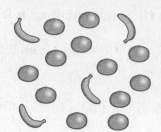

2. **MODEL TRAINS** Hiroshi has 4 engines and 18 box cars. Find the ratio of engines to box cars. Write the ratio as a fraction in simplest form. Then explain its meaning.

3. **ZOOS** A petting zoo has 5 lambs, 11 rabbits, 4 goats, and 4 piglets. Find the ratio of goats to the total number of animals. Then explain its meaning.

4. **FOOD** At the potluck, there were 6 pecan pies, 7 lemon pies, 13 cherry pies, and 8 apple pies. Find the ratio of apple pies to the total number of pies. Then explain its meaning.

Write each rate as a unit rate.

5. 3 inches of snow in 6 hours

6. $46 for 5 toys

7. **TRAINS** The Nozomi train in Japan can travel 558 miles in 3 hours. At this rate, how far can the train travel per hour?

ANALYZE TABLES For Exercises 8 and 9, refer to the table showing tide pool animals.

8. Find the ratio of limpets to snails. Then explain its meaning.

Animals Found in a Tide Pool	
Animal	**Number**
Anemones	11
Limpets	14
Snails	18
Starfish	9

9. Find the ratio of snails to the total number of animals. Then explain its meaning.

6-1 Word Problem Practice

Ratios and Rates

1. FOOTBALL In a recent the NFL season, the Miami Dolphins won 4 games and the Oakland Raiders won 5 games. What is the ratio of wins for the Dolphins to wins for the Raiders?

2. GARDENING Rod has 10 rosebushes, 2 of which produce yellow roses. Write the ratio *2 yellow rosebushes out of 10 rosebushes* in simplest form.

3. TENNIS Nancy and Lisa played 20 sets of tennis. Nancy won 12 of them. Write the ratio of Nancy's wins to the total number of sets in simplest form.

4. AGES Oscar is 16 years old and his sister Julia is 12 years old. What will be the ratio of Oscar's age to Julia's age in 2 years? Write as a fraction in simplest form.

5. MOVIES Four friends paid a total of $32 for movie tickets. What is the ratio *$32 for 4 people* written as a unit rate?

6. WORKING At a warehouse, the employees can unload 18 trucks in 6 hours. What is the unit rate for unloading trucks?

7. ANIMALS A reindeer can run 96 miles in 3 hours. At this rate, how far can a reindeer run in 1 hour? Explain.

8. SHOPPING Jenny wants to buy cereal that comes in large and small boxes. The 32-ounce box costs $4.16, and the 14-ounce box costs $2.38. Which box is less expensive per ounce? Explain.

Lesson 6-1

6-1 Enrichment

Ratios and Rectangles

1. Use a centimeter ruler to measure the width and the length of each rectangle. Then express the ratio of the width to the length as a fraction in simplest form.

A

B

C

D

E

2. Similar figures have the same shape, but not necessarily the same size. Two rectangles are similar if the ratio of the width to the length is the same for each. Which rectangles in Exercise 1 are similar?

3. For centuries artists and architects have used a shape called the **golden rectangle** because people seem to find it most pleasant to look at. In a golden rectangle, the ratio of the width to the length is a little less than $\frac{5}{8}$. Which rectangle in Exercise 1 is most nearly a golden rectangle?

6-2 Lesson Reading Guide

Ratio Tables

Get Ready for the Lesson

Read the introduction at the top of page 322 in your textbook. Write your answers below.

1. How many cans of juice and how many cans of water would you need to make 2 batches that have the same taste? 3 batches? Draw a picture to support your answers.

2. Find the ratio in simplest form of juice to water needed for 1, 2, and 3 batches of juice. What do you notice?

Read the Lesson

3. In a ratio table, what relationship exists between the columns?

4. Explain how you can check your answers when using a ratio table to solve a problem.

Remember What You Learned

5. Think of a real-world situation in which you would need to find equivalent ratios. Make a ratio table for this situation. Would you need to *scale back* or *scale forward* in this situation to find equivalent ratios? Explain.

Lesson 6-2

6-2 Study Guide and Intervention

Ratio Tables

A **ratio table** organizes data into columns that are filled with pairs of numbers that have the same ratio, or are equivalent. **Equivalent ratios** express the same relationship between two quantities.

Example 1   BAKING You need 1 cup of rolled oats to make 24 oatmeal cookies. Use the ratio table at the right to find how many oatmeal cookies you can make with 5 cups of rolled oats.

Cups of Oats	1				5
Oatmeal Cookies	24				■

Find a pattern and extend it.

+1 +1 +1 +1

Cups of Oats	1	2	3	4	5
Oatmeal Cookies	24	48	72	96	120

+24 +24 +24 +24

So, 120 oatmeal cookies can be made with 5 cups of rolled oats.

Multiplying or dividing two related quantities by the same number is called **scaling**. You may sometimes need to *scale back* and then *scale forward* or vice versa to find an equivalent ratio.

Example 2   SHOPPING A department store has socks on sale for 4 pairs for $10. Use the ratio table at the right to find the cost of 6 pairs of socks.

Pairs of Socks		4	6
Cost in Dollars		10	■

There is no whole number by which you can multiply 4 to get 6. Instead, scale back to 2 and then forward to 6.

So, the cost of 6 pairs of socks would be $15.

× 3
÷ 2

Pairs of Socks	2	4	6
Cost in Dollars	5	10	15

÷ 2
× 3

Exercises

1. **EXERCISE** Keewan bikes 6 miles in 30 minutes. At this rate, how long would it take him to bike 18 miles?

Distance Biked (mi)	6		18
Time (min)	30		■

2. **HOBBIES** Christine is making fleece blankets. 6 yards of fleece will make 2 blankets. How many blankets can she make with 9 yards of fleece?

Yards of Fleece		6	9
Number of Blankets		2	■

6-2 Skills Practice

Ratio Tables

For Exercises 1–4, use the ratio table given to solve each problem.

1. **BAKING** A recipe for 1 apple pie calls for 6 cups of sliced apples. How many cups of sliced apples are needed to make 4 apple pies?

Number of Pies	1			4
Cups of Sliced Apples	6			■

2. **BASEBALL CARDS** Justin bought 40 packs of baseball cards for a discounted price of $64. If he sells 10 packs of baseball cards to a friend at cost, how much should he charge?

Number of Baseball Card Packs	10		40
Cost in Dollars	■		64

3. **SOUP** A recipe that yields 12 cups of soup calls for 28 ounces of beef broth. How many ounces of beef broth do you need to make 18 cups of the soup?

Number of Cups		12	18
Ounces of Beef Broth		28	■

4. **ANIMALS** At a dog shelter, a 24-pound bag of dog food will feed 36 dogs a day. How many dogs would you expect to feed with a 16-pound bag of dog food?

Pounds of Dog Food	16	24	
Number of Dogs Fed	■	36	

5. **AUTOMOBILES** Mr. Fink's economy car can travel 420 miles on a 12-gallon tank of gas. Use a ratio table to determine how many miles he can travel on 8 gallons.

Miles	420		■
Gallons	12		8

Lesson 6-2

6-2 Practice

Ratio Tables

For Exercises 1–3, use the ratio tables given to solve each problem.

1. **CAMPING** To disinfect 1 quart of stream water to make it drinkable, you need to add 2 tablets of iodine. How many tablets do you need to disinfect 4 quarts?

Number of Tablets	2			■
Number of Quarts	1			4

2. **BOOKS** A book store bought 160 copies of a book from the publisher for $4,000. If the store gives away 2 books, how much money will it lose?

Number of Copies	160		2
Cost in Dollars	4,000		■

3. **BIRDS** An ostrich can run at a rate of 50 miles in 60 minutes. At this rate, how long would it take an ostrich to run 18 miles?

Distance Run (mi)	50		18
Time (min)	60		■

4. **DISTANCE** If 10 miles is about 16 kilometers and the distance between two towns is 45 miles, use a ratio table to find the distance between the towns in kilometers. Explain your reasoning.

5. **SALARY** Luz earns $400 for 40 hours of work. Use a ratio table to determine how much she earns for 6 hours of work.

RECIPES For Exercises 6–8, use the following information.

A soup that serves 16 people calls for 2 cans of chopped clams, 4 cups of chicken broth, 6 cups of milk, and 4 cups of cubed potatoes.

6. Create a ratio table to represent this situation.

7. How much of each ingredient would you need to make an identical recipe that serves 8 people? 32 people?

8. How much of each ingredient would you need to make an identical recipe that serves 24 people? Explain your reasoning.

6-2 Word Problem Practice

Ratio Tables

For Exercises 1–4, use the ratio tables below.

Table 1

Cups of Flour	1			
Number of Cookies	30			

Table 2

Number of Books	6	
Cost in Dollars	10	

1. **BAKING** In Table 1, how many cookies could you make with 4 cups of flour?

2. **BAKING** In Table 1, how many cups of flour would you need to make 90 cookies?

3. **BOOKS** In Table 2, at this rate how many books can you buy with $5?

4. **BOOKS** In Table 2, at this rate, how much would it cost to buy 9 books?

5. **FRUIT** Patrick buys 12 bunches of bananas for $9 for the after school program. Use a ratio table to determine how much Patrick will pay for 8 bunches of bananas.

6. **HIKING** On a hiking trip, LaShana notes that she hikes about 12 kilometers every 4 hours. If she continues at this rate, use a ratio table to determine about how many kilometers she could hike in 6 hours.

Lesson 6-2

6-2 Enrichment

Business Planning

In order to have a successful business, the manager must plan ahead and decide how certain actions will affect the business. The first step is to predict the financial impact of business decisions. Julie has decided that she wants to start a brownie business to make extra money over the summer. Before she can ask her parents for money to start her business, she needs to have some information about how many batches of brownies she can make in a day and for how much she must sell the brownies to make a profit.

1. Julie can bake 3 batches of brownies in 2 hours. Her goal is to bake 12 batches of brownies each day. Use the table to find how many hours Julie will need to bake to reach her goal.

Batches of Brownies	3			12
Hours	2			

2. Each batch of brownies will be sold for $2.00. How much money will Julie make if she sells 6 batches of brownies?

Batches of Brownies	1					6
Cost	$2					

3. If Julie works for 10 hours a day, how many batches of brownies can she bake?

Batches of Brownies	3	
Hours	2	10

4. Julie hires a friend to help. Together, they can bake 24 batches of brownies in 8 hours. How long does it take for the two of them to bake 6 batches of brownies?

Batches of Brownies	6			24
Hours				8

5. If Julie and her friend can bake 24 batches of brownies in 8 hours, and they both work 40 hours in one week, how many batches of brownies can they bake that week? If Julie still charges $2.00 a batch, how much money will they make that week?

Hours	8			40
Batches of Brownies	24			

Batches of Brownies	1	
Cost	$2	

6-3 Lesson Reading Guide

Proportions

Get Ready for the Lesson

Read the introduction at the top of page 329 in your textbook. Write your answers below.

1. Express the relationship between the total cost and number of prints he made for each situation as a rate in fraction form.

2. Compare the relationship between the numerators of each rate you wrote in Exercise 1. Compare the relationship between the denominators of these rates.

3. Are the rates you wrote in Exercise 1 equivalent? Explain.

Read the Lesson

4. Look at the Key Concept box on page 329. How can you tell that the two examples given are proportions?

5. Explain one method you can use to determine if a relationship among quantities is proportional.

Remember What You Learned

6. Work with a partner. Each of you should write about two different relationships, one which is proportional, and one that is not. Exchange what you wrote with your partner. Then determine which relationship is proportional and which one is not proportional.

Lesson 6-3

6-3 Study Guide and Intervention

Proportions

Two quantities are said to be **proportional** if they have a constant ratio. A **proportion** is an equation stating that two ratios are equivalent.

Example 1 Determine if the quantities in each pair of rates are proportional. Explain your reasoning and express each proportional relationship as a proportion.

$35 for 7 balls of yarn; $24 for 4 balls of yarn.

Write each ratio as a fraction. Then find its unit rate.

$$\frac{\$35}{7 \text{ balls of yarn}} \overset{\div 7}{\underset{\div 7}{=}} \frac{\$5}{1 \text{ ball of yarn}} \qquad \frac{\$24}{4 \text{ balls of yarn}} \overset{\div 4}{\underset{\div 4}{=}} \frac{\$6}{1 \text{ ball of yarn}}$$

Since the ratios do not share the same unit rate, the cost is not proportional to the number of balls of yarn purchased.

Example 2 Determine if the quantities in each pair of rates are proportional. Explain your reasoning and express each proportional relationship as a proportion.

8 boys out of 24 students; 4 boys out of 12 students

Write each ratio as a fraction.

$$\frac{8 \text{ boys}}{24 \text{ students}} \overset{\div 2}{\underset{\div 2}{\frown}} \frac{4 \text{ boys}}{12 \text{ students}} \quad \leftarrow \text{The numerator and the denominator are divided by the same number.}$$

Since the fractions are equivalent, the number of boys is proportional to the number of students.

Exercises

Determine if the quantities in each pair of rates are proportional. Explain your reasoning and express each proportional relationship as a proportion.

1. $12 saved after 2 weeks; $36 saved after 6 weeks

2. $9 for 3 magazines; $20 for 5 magazines

3. 135 miles driven in 3 hours; 225 miles driven in 5 hours

4. 24 computers for 30 students; 48 computers for 70 students

6-3 Skills Practice

Proportions

Determine if the quantities in each pair of ratios or rates are proportional. Explain your reasoning and express each proportional relationship as a proportion.

1. $18 for 3 bracelets; $30 for 5 bracelets

2. 120 calories in 2 servings; 360 calories in 6 servings

3. 4 hours worked for $12; 7 hours worked for $28

4. 15 blank CDs for $5; 45 blank CDs for $15

5. 24 points scored in 4 games; 48 points scored in 10 games

6. 15 out of 20 students own hand-held games; 105 out of 160 students own hand-held games.

7. 30 minutes to jog 3 miles; 50 minutes to jog 5 miles

8. $3 for 6 muffins; $9 for 18 muffins

9. 360 miles driven on 12 gallons of fuel; 270 miles driven on 9 gallons of fuel

10. 2 pairs of jeans for $50; 4 pairs of jeans for $90

Lesson 6-3

6-3 Practice

Proportions

Determine if the quantities in each pair of ratios are proportional. Explain your reasoning and express each proportional relationship as a proportion.

1. 18 vocabulary words learned in 2 hours; 27 vocabulary words learned in 3 hours

2. $15 for 5 pairs of socks; $25 for 10 pairs of socks

3. 20 out of 45 students attended the concert; 12 out of 25 students attended the concert

4. 78 correct answers out of 100 test questions; 39 correct answers out of 50 test questions

5. 15 minutes to drive 21 miles; 25 minutes to drive 35 miles

ANIMALS For Exercises 6–8, refer to the table on lengths of some animals with long tails. Determine if each pair of animals has the same body length to tail length proportions. Explain your reasoning.

Animal Lengths (mm)		
Animal	**Head & Body**	**Tail**
Brown Rat	240	180
Hamster	250	50
Lemming	125	25
Opossum	480	360
Prairie Dog	280	40

6. brown rat and opossum

7. hamster and lemming

8. opossum and prairie dog

6-3 Word Problem Practice

Proportions

1. **FITNESS** Jessica can do 60 jumping-jacks in 2 minutes. Juanita can do 150 jumping-jacks in 5 minutes. Are these rates proportional? Explain your reasoning.

2. **BAKING** A cookie recipe that yields 48 cookies calls for 2 cups of flour. A different cookie recipe that yields 60 cookies calls for 3 cups of flour. Are these rates proportional? Explain your reasoning.

3. **MUSIC** A music store is having a sale where you can buy 2 new-release CDs for $22 or you can buy 4 new-release CDs for $40. Are these rates proportional? Explain your reasoning.

4. **TRAVEL** On the Mertler's vacation to Florida, they drove 180 miles in 3 hours before stopping for lunch. After lunch they drove 120 miles in 2 hours before stopping for gas. Are these rates proportional? Explain your reasoning.

5. **BOOKS** At the school book sale, Michael bought 3 books for $6. Darnell bought 5 books for $10. Are these rates proportional? Explain your reasoning.

6. **SURVEY** One school survey showed that 3 out of 5 students own a pet. Another survey showed that 6 out of 11 students own a pet. Are these results proportional? Explain your reasoning.

Lesson 6-3

6-3 Enrichment

"Liberty Enlightening the World"

On July 4, 1889, in gratitude to the French for the gift of the Statue of Liberty, Americans from Paris gave to the French a miniature Statue of Liberty. The statue is made of bronze and is approximately one fourth the size of the original. This smaller-scale copy is found near the Grenelle Bridge on the Île des Cygnes, an island in the Seine River about one mile south of the Eiffel Tower.

1. If the original Statue of Liberty is approximately 150 feet tall, about how tall is the replica?

2. Complete the table. The first one is done for you.

	Original Statue of Liberty	Replica
Length of hand	16 ft	4 ft
Length of nose	4.5 ft	
Length of right arm	42 ft	
Head thickness from ear to ear		2.5 ft
Width of mouth		9 in.
Thickness of waist	35 ft	
Distance from heel to the top of her head	111 ft	
Length of index finger	8 ft	
Circumference of the second joint	3.5 ft	

3. The fingernail on the index finger of the original weighs 1.5 kilograms. How much does the fingernail on the replica in France weigh?

4. The dimensions of the tablet that Lady Liberty is holding are 23.6 feet by 13.6 feet by 2 feet. What are the dimensions of the smaller-scale tablet in France?

5. **CHALLENGE** The fingernail on the index finger is 13 inches long and 10 inches wide. What will be the area of the fingernail on the replica in France?

6-3 TI-73 Activity

Proportions

Cara and Jeff are going to cater a family reunion. Their recipe for potato salad serves 10 people. How much of each ingredient will they need to make enough for 75 people? You can use lists on your calculator to find the amount of each ingredient.

Mustard Potato Salad	
$\frac{1}{2}$ c light mayonnaise	$\frac{1}{4}$ t salt
2 T Dijon mustard	$\frac{1}{8}$ t pepper
2 T sweet pickle relish	5 c cooked potatoes
1 T white vinegar	$\frac{1}{4}$ c minced parsley

Combine the first six ingredients in a large bowl. Add potatoes and toss. Cover and chill overnight. Garnish with parsley. Serves 10.

Example 1

Step 1 Clear all lists.

2nd [MEM] 6 ENTER

Open the List feature.

LIST

Step 2 Enter the recipe ingredient amounts in L1.

Use the b⁄c key to enter fractions. Press ENTER after each value.

Step 3 Enter a formula in L2 to find the amount for 75 people. Use a proportion.

$$\frac{\text{Recipe Amount}}{10 \text{ people}} = \frac{x}{75 \text{ people}}$$

$$10x = (\text{Recipe Amount}) \times 75$$

$$x = (\text{Recipe Amount}) \times 75 \div 10 \quad \text{or} \quad x = \text{L1} \times 75 \div 10$$

Use ▶ and ▲ to move to L2. Be sure you are on L2 and not L2(1).

Enter the formula.

2nd [TEXT] " Done ENTER 2nd [STAT] 1 × 75 ÷ 10 2nd [TEXT]

" Done ENTER ENTER

The amounts for 75 people are shown in L2. The amount of mayonnaise is $3\frac{3}{4}$ cups.

Exercises

Solve the following proportion questions.

1. Suppose you need to make enough potato salad for 45 people. Enter a new formula in L3 and find the amounts you need. Record the formula. List the amount of each ingredient.

2. Suppose you decide that the original recipe would serve 12 people. You need to feed 30 people. Enter a new formula in L4 to find the amounts you need. Record the formula. List the amount of each ingredient.

Lesson 6-3

Copyright © Glencoe/McGraw-Hill, a division of The McGraw-Hill Companies, Inc.

6-4 Lesson Reading Guide

Algebra: Solving Proportions

Get Ready for the Lesson

**Read the introduction at the top of page 334 in your textbook.
Write your answers below.**

1. How many pairs of flip flops can you buy with $20? $25?

2. Write a proportion to express the relationship between the cost of 3 pairs of flip flops and the cost c of 7 pairs of flip flops.

3. How much will it cost to buy 6 pairs of flip flops?

Read the Lesson

4. In Example 1, explain why you multiply by 5 to solve the proportion.

5. Look at the final sentence in Example 4 on page 335—"So, about 400 out of 500 people can be expected to prefer eating at a restaurant." Why is it important to use *can be expected* in this answer?

Remember What You Learned

6. Work with a partner. Study Examples 1–3 on pages 334 and 335. Write a proportion that needs to be solved for an unknown value. Exchange proportions and solve for the unknown value. Explain how you arrived at your solution.

6-4 Study Guide and Intervention

Algebra: Solving Proportions

To *solve a proportion* means to find the unknown value in the proportion. By examining how the numerators or denominators of the proportion are related, you can perform an operation on one fraction to create an equivalent fraction.

Example 1 Solve $\frac{3}{4} = \frac{b}{12}$.

Find a value for b that would make the fractions equivalent.

$$\overset{\times\,3}{\frac{3}{4} = \frac{b}{12}}_{\times\,3} \qquad \text{Since } 4 \times 3 = 12, \text{ multiply the numerator and denominator by 3.}$$

$b = 3 \times 3$ or 9

Example 2 NUTRITION Three servings of broccoli contain 150 calories. How many servings of broccoli contain 250 calories?

Set up the proportion. Let a represent the number of servings that contain 250 calories.

$$\frac{150 \text{ calories}}{3 \text{ servings}} = \frac{250 \text{ calories}}{a \text{ servings}}$$

Find the unit rate.

$$\overset{\div\,3}{\frac{150 \text{ calories}}{3 \text{ servings}} = \frac{50 \text{ calories}}{1 \text{ serving}}}_{\div\,3}$$

Rewrite the proportion using the unit rate and solve using equivalent fractions.

$$\overset{\times\,5}{\frac{50 \text{ calories}}{1 \text{ serving}} = \frac{250 \text{ calories}}{5 \text{ servings}}}_{\times\,5}$$

So, 5 servings of broccoli contain 250 calories.

Exercises

Solve each proportion.

1. $\frac{2}{3} = \frac{8}{n}$

2. $\frac{2}{4} = \frac{y}{8}$

3. $\frac{3}{5} = \frac{b}{15}$

4. $\frac{4}{5} = \frac{16}{w}$

5. $\frac{d}{16} = \frac{3}{8}$

6. $\frac{2}{y} = \frac{6}{9}$

7. **MUSIC** Jeremy spent $33 on 3 CDs. At this rate, how much would 5 CDs cost?

Lesson 6-4

6-4 Skills Practice

Algebra: Solving Proportions

Solve each proportion.

1. $\dfrac{2}{5} = \dfrac{8}{x}$

2. $\dfrac{2}{7} = \dfrac{4}{y}$

3. $\dfrac{3}{5} = \dfrac{b}{30}$

4. $\dfrac{2}{9} = \dfrac{c}{36}$

5. $\dfrac{4}{5} = \dfrac{d}{25}$

6. $\dfrac{20}{4} = \dfrac{10}{f}$

7. $\dfrac{g}{2} = \dfrac{28}{14}$

8. $\dfrac{2}{x} = \dfrac{10}{25}$

9. $\dfrac{4}{3} = \dfrac{h}{18}$

10. $\dfrac{10}{30} = \dfrac{2}{r}$

11. $\dfrac{t}{18} = \dfrac{3}{6}$

12. $\dfrac{2}{3} = \dfrac{6}{m}$

13. $\dfrac{9}{2} = \dfrac{s}{6}$

14. $\dfrac{n}{36} = \dfrac{2}{6}$

15. $\dfrac{4}{u} = \dfrac{12}{21}$

16. $\dfrac{5}{6} = \dfrac{m}{12}$

17. $\dfrac{d}{27} = \dfrac{4}{9}$

18. $\dfrac{5}{8} = \dfrac{15}{q}$

19. $\dfrac{15}{27} = \dfrac{5}{k}$

20. $\dfrac{4}{x} = \dfrac{20}{30}$

21. $\dfrac{b}{3} = \dfrac{24}{9}$

22. $\dfrac{z}{35} = \dfrac{4}{7}$

23. $\dfrac{6}{c} = \dfrac{24}{28}$

24. $\dfrac{6}{8} = \dfrac{x}{24}$

25. $\dfrac{14}{16} = \dfrac{b}{8}$

26. $\dfrac{8}{r} = \dfrac{24}{27}$

27. $\dfrac{16}{36} = \dfrac{t}{9}$

6-4 Practice

Algebra: Solving Proportions

Solve each proportion.

1. $\dfrac{2}{3} = \dfrac{n}{21}$

2. $\dfrac{2}{x} = \dfrac{16}{40}$

3. $\dfrac{80}{100} = \dfrac{b}{5}$

4. $\dfrac{m}{2} = \dfrac{75}{50}$

5. $\dfrac{6}{5} = \dfrac{42}{a}$

6. $\dfrac{3}{d} = \dfrac{21}{56}$

7. $\dfrac{4}{3} = \dfrac{f}{45}$

8. $\dfrac{h}{12} = \dfrac{70}{120}$

9. $\dfrac{3}{5} = \dfrac{27}{p}$

10. $\dfrac{26}{21} = \dfrac{r}{63}$

11. $\dfrac{17}{y} = \dfrac{102}{222}$

12. $\dfrac{7}{10} = \dfrac{c}{25}$

13. **MAMMALS** A pronghorn antelope can travel 105 miles in 3 hours. If it continued traveling at the same speed, how far could a pronghorn travel in 11 hours?

14. **BIKES** Out of 32 students in a class, 5 said they ride their bikes to school. Based on these results, predict how many of the 800 students in the school ride their bikes to school.

15. **MEAT** Hamburger sells for 3 pounds for $6. If Alicia buys 10 pounds of hamburger, how much will she pay?

16. **FOOD** If 24 extra large cans of soup will serve 96 people, how many cans should Ann buy to serve 28 people?

17. **BIRDS** The ruby throated hummingbird has a wing beat of about 200 beats per second. About how many wing beats would a hummingbird have in 3 minutes?

Lesson 6-4

6-4 Word Problem Practice

Algebra: Solving Proportions

1. SCHOOL The ratio of boys to girls in history class is 4 to 5. How many girls are in the class if there are 12 boys in the class? Explain.

2. FACTORIES A factory produces 6 motorcycles in 9 hours. Write a proportion and solve it to find how many hours it takes to produce 16 motorcycles.

3. READING James read 4 pages in a book in 6 minutes. How long would you expect him to take to read 6 pages?

4. COOKING A recipe that will make 3 pies calls for 7 cups of flour. Write a proportion and solve it to find how many pies can be made with 28 cups of flour.

5. TYPING Sara can type 90 words in 4 minutes. About how many words would you expect her to type in 10 minutes?

6. BASKETBALL The Lakewood Wildcats won 5 of their first 7 games this year. There are 28 games in the season. About how many games would you expect the Wildcats to win this season? Explain your reasoning.

7. FOOD Two slices of Dan's Famous Pizza have 230 Calories. How many Calories would you expect to be in 5 slices of the same pizza?

8. SHOPPING Andy paid $12 for 4 baseball card packs. Write a proportion and solve it to find how many baseball card packs he can purchase for $21.

6-4 Enrichment

Ada

Did you know that a woman wrote the first description of a computer programming language? She was the daughter of a famous English lord and was born in 1815. She had a deep understanding of mathematics and was fascinated by calculating machines. Her interests led her to create the first algorithm. In 1843, she translated a French version of a lecture by Charles Babbage. In her notes to the translation, she outlined the fundamental concepts of computer programming. She died in 1852. In 1979, the U.S. Department of Defense named the computer language *Ada* after her.

To find out this woman's full name, solve the proportion for each letter.

1. $\frac{7}{A} = \frac{28}{40}$ 2. $\frac{5}{4} = \frac{B}{36}$ 3. $\frac{1}{3} = \frac{C}{15}$

4. $\frac{5}{D} = \frac{35}{63}$ 5. $\frac{2}{5} = \frac{E}{20}$ 6. $\frac{2}{18} = \frac{L}{27}$

7. $\frac{6}{N} = \frac{12}{14}$ 8. $\frac{9}{11} = \frac{O}{44}$ 9. $\frac{2}{8} = \frac{R}{4}$

10. $\frac{5}{V} = \frac{25}{30}$ 11. $\frac{7}{4} = \frac{Y}{28}$

Now look for each solution below. Write the corresponding letter on the line above the solution. If you have calculated correctly, the letters will spell her name.

$\overline{10}$ $\overline{9}$ $\overline{10}$ $\overline{45}$ $\overline{49}$ $\overline{1}$ $\overline{36}$ $\overline{7}$

$\overline{3}$ $\overline{36}$ $\overline{6}$ $\overline{8}$ $\overline{3}$ $\overline{10}$ $\overline{5}$ $\overline{8}$

Lesson 6-4

6-5 Study Guide and Intervention

Problem-Solving Investigation: Look for a Pattern

When solving problems, one strategy that is helpful is to *look for a pattern*. In some problem situations, you can extend and examine a pattern in order to solve the problem.

You can use the *look for a pattern* strategy, along with the following four-step problem solving plan to solve a problem.

1 Understand – Read and get a general understanding of the problem.

2 Plan – Make a plan to solve the problem and estimate the solution.

3 Solve – Use your plan to solve the problem.

4 Check – Check the reasonableness of your solution.

Example   MEDICINE Monisha has the flu. The doctor gave her medicine to take over the next 2 weeks. The first 3 days she is to take 2 pills a day. Then the remaining days she is to take 1 pill. How many pills will Monisha have taken at the end of the 2 weeks?

Understand You know she is to take the medicine for 2 weeks. You also know she is to take 2 pills the first 3 days and then only 1 pill the remaining days. You need to find the total number of pills.

Plan Start with the first week and look for a pattern.

Solve

Day	1	2	3	4	5	6	7
Number of Pills	2	2	2	1	1	1	1
Total Pills	2	2 + 2 = 4	4 + 2 = 6	6 + 1 = 7	7 + 1 = 8	8 + 1 = 9	9 + 1 = 10

After the first few days the number of pills increases by 1. You can add 7 more pills to the total for the first week, 10 + 7 = 17. So, by the end of the 2 weeks, Monisha will have taken 17 pills to get over the flu.

Check You can extend the table for the next 7 days to check the answer.

Exercise

TIME Buses arrive every 30 minutes at the bus stop. The first bus arrives at 6:20 A.M. Hogan wants to get on the first bus after 8:00 A.M. What time will the bus that Hogan wants to take arrive at the bus stop?

6-5 Skills Practice

Problem-Solving Investigation: Look for a Pattern

Solve. Use the look for a pattern strategy.

1. **NUMBER SENSE** Describe the pattern below, Then find the missing number.

    1, 20, 400, ___?___, 160,000

2. **GEOMETRY** Use the pattern below to find the perimeter of the eighth figure.

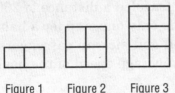

    Figure 1   Figure 2   Figure 3

3. **PHYSICAL SCIENCE** A cup of marbles hangs from a rubber band. The length of the rubber band is measured as shown in the graph at the right. Predict the approximate length of the rubber band if 6 marbles are in the cup.

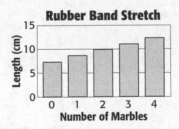

4. **ALLOWANCE** In 2002, Estella earned $200 in allowance, and Kelsey earned $150 in allowance. Each year Kelsey earned $20 more in allowance, and Estella earned $10 more. In what year will they earn the same amount of money? How much will it be?

Lesson 6-5

6-5 Practice

Problem-Solving Investigation: Look for a Pattern

Mixed Problem Solving

Use the look for a pattern strategy to solve Exercises 1 and 2.

1. **MONEY** In 2005, Trey had $7,200 in his saving-for-college account and Juan had $8,000. Each year, Trey will add $400 and Juan will add $200. In what year will they both have the same amount of money in their accounts, not counting interest earned? How much will it be?

2. **BUTTONS** Draw the next two figures in the pattern below.

Use any strategy to solve Exercises 3–7. Some strategies are shown below.

Problem-Solving Strategies
• Guess and check.
• Look for a pattern.
• Act it out.

3. **MUSIC** Last week Jason practiced playing his bassoon for 95 minutes. This week he practiced 5 more minutes than 3 times the number of minutes he practiced last week. How many minutes did Jason practice this week?

4. **NUMBER SENSE** Describe the pattern below. Then find the missing number.

   5,000, 2,500, ■, 625, . . .

5. **TRAVEL** An express bus left the station at 6:30 a.m. and arrived at its destination at 12:00 noon. It traveled a distance of 260 miles and made only one stop for a half hour to drop off and pick up passengers. What was the average speed of the bus?

6. **MONEY** Len bought a $24.99 pair of pants and paid a total of $27.05, including tax. How much was the tax?

7. **PHOTOGRAPHY** Ms. Julian gives photography workshops. She collected $540 in fees for a workshop attended by 12 participants. Ms. Julian spent $15 per person for supplies for them and herself and $6 per person for box lunches for them and herself. How much money did Ms. Julian have left as profit?

6-5 Word Problem Practice

Problem-Solving Investigation: Look for a Pattern

1. HEIGHT Fernando is 2 inches taller than Jason. Jason is 1.5 inches shorter than Kendra and 1 inch taller than Nicole. Hao, who is 5 feet 10 inches tall, is 2.5 inches taller than Fernando. How tall is each student?

2. FRUIT The table below shows the results of a survey of students' favorite fruit. How many more students like apples than bananas?

Favorite Fruit							
A	B	G	B	A	B	A	O
O	A	G	G	G	A	A	B
G	O	A	B	O	B	O	O

A = apple   B = banana   G = grapes
O = orange

3. MONEY Dominic's mother gave him $20 to go to the grocery store. If the groceries cost $12.56, how much change will he receive?

4. BOOKS An author has written 4 different books. Each book is available in hard bound, soft bound, and on tape. How many different items are available by this author?

5. FOOTBALL The varsity football team scored 24 points in last Friday's game. They scored a combination of 7-point touchdowns and 3-point field goals. How many touchdowns and how many field goals did they score?

6. CYCLING Jody and Lazaro are cycling in a 24-mile race. Jody is cycling at an average speed of 8 miles per hour. Lazaro is cycling at an average speed of 6 miles per hour. If they both started the race at the same time, who will finish first? How much faster will they finish the race?

Lesson 6-5

6-6 Lesson Reading Guide

Sequences and Expressions

Get Ready for the Lesson

**Read the introduction at the top of page 343 in your textbook.
Write your answers below.**

1. Find the rate of slices to the number of pizzas for each row in the table.

2. Is the number of pizzas proportional to the number of slices? Explain your reasoning.

3. Make an ordered list of the number of slices and describe the pattern between consecutive numbers in this list.

4. What relationship appears to exist between the pattern found in Exercise 3 and the rates found in Exercise 1?

Read the Lesson

5. If you have a list of numbers, how can you tell if they are an arithmetic sequence?

6. In extending a sequence, how can you use an algebraic expression to find the tenth term?

Remember What You Learned

7. Work with a partner. Make up a sequence of numbers that follow a certain pattern. Exchange lists with your partner. For the list you receive from your partner, describe the pattern, write a function describing the pattern, and then find the tenth term in the pattern.

6-6 Study Guide and Intervention

Sequences and Expressions

A **sequence** is a list of numbers in a specific order. Each number in the sequence is called a **term**. An **arithmetic sequence** is a sequence in which each term is found by adding the same number to the previous term.

Example Use words and symbols to describe the value of each term as a function of its position. Then find the value of the tenth term in the sequence.

Position	1	2	3	4	n
Value of Term	4	8	12	16	?

Study the relationship between each position and the value of its term.

Notice that the value of each term is 4 times its position number. So the value of the term in position n is $4n$.

To find the value of the tenth term, replace n with 10 in the algebraic expression $4n$. Since $4 \times 10 = 40$, the value of the tenth term in the sequence is 40.

Position		Value of term
1	$\times\, 4 =$	4
2	$\times\, 4 =$	8
3	$\times\, 4 =$	12
4	$\times\, 4 =$	16
n	$\times\, 4 =$	$4n$

Exercises

Use words and symbols to describe the value of each term as a function of its position. Then find the value of the tenth term in the sequence.

1.

Position	3	4	5	6	n
Value of Term	1	2	3	4	?

2.

Position	1	2	3	4	n
Value of Term	5	10	15	20	?

3.

Position	4	5	6	7	n
Value of Term	11	12	13	14	?

6-6 Skills Practice

Sequences and Expressions

Use words and symbols to describe the value of each term as a function of its position. Then find the value of the tenth term in the sequence.

1.

Position	5	6	7	8	n
Value of Term	2	3	4	5	?

2.

Position	1	2	3	4	n
Value of Term	6	12	18	24	?

3.

Position	1	2	3	4	n
Value of Term	10	11	12	13	?

4.

Position	1	2	3	4	n
Value of Term	4	8	12	16	?

5.

Position	5	6	7	8	n
Value of Term	0	1	2	3	?

6.

Position	2	4	6	8	n
Value of Term	14	16	18	20	?

7.

Position	5	6	7	8	n
Value of Term	1	2	3	4	?

8.

Position	1	2	3	4	n
Value of Term	11	22	33	44	?

6-6 Practice

Sequences and Expressions

Use words and symbols to describe the value of each term as a function of its position. Then find the value of the sixteenth term in the sequence.

1.

Position	2	3	4	5	n
Value of Term	8	12	16	20	■

2.

Position	8	9	10	11	n
Value of Term	14	15	16	17	■

3.

Position	11	12	13	14	n
Value of Term	4	5	6	7	■

4.

Position	21	22	23	24	n
Value of Term	12	13	14	15	■

Determine how the next term in each sequence can be found. Then find the next two terms in the sequence.

5. 3, 16, 29, 42, …

6. 29, 25, 21, 17, …

7. 1.2, 3.5, 5.8, 8.1, …

Find the missing number in each sequence.

8. 5, ■, 10, $12\frac{1}{2}$, …

9. 11.5, 9.4, ■, 5.2

10. 40, ■, $37\frac{1}{3}$, 36, …

11. **MEASUREMENT** There are 52 weeks in 1 year. In the space at the right, make a table and write an algebraic expression relating the number of weeks to the number of years. Then find Hana's age in weeks if she is 11 years old.

12. **COMPUTERS** There are about 8 bits of digital information in 1 byte. In the space at the right, make a table and write an algebraic expression relating the number of bits to the number of bytes. Then find the number of bits there are in one kilobyte if there are 1,024 bytes in one kilobyte.

6-6 Word Problem Practice

Sequences and Expressions

1. **AGE** There are 12 months in 1 year. If Juan is 11 years old, how many months old is he? Make a table then write an algebraic expression relating the number of months to the number of years.

2. **MEASUREMENT** There are 12 inches in 1 foot. The height of Rachel's door is 7 feet. Find the height in inches. Make a table then write an algebraic expression relating the number of feet to inches.

3. **RUNNING** There are 60 seconds in 1 minute. Pete can run all the way around the track in 180 seconds. Find how long it takes Pete to run around the track in minutes. Make a table then write an algebraic expression relating the number of seconds to the number of minutes.

4. **FRUIT** There are 16 ounces in 1 pound. Chanda picked 9 pounds of cherries from her tree this year. Find the number of ounces of cherries Chanda picked. Make a table then write an algebraic expression relating the number of ounces to the number of pounds.

5. **SPORTS** There are 3 feet in 1 yard. Tanya Streeter holds the world record for free-diving in the ocean. She dove 525 feet in $3\frac{1}{2}$ minutes. Find the number of yards she dove. Make a table then write an algebraic expression relating the number of feet to the number of yards.

6. **COOKING** There are 8 fluid ounces in 1 cup. A beef stew recipe calls for 3 cups of vegetable juice. Find the number of fluid ounces of vegetable juice needed for the recipe. Make a table then write an algebraic expression relating the number of fluid ounces to the number of cups.

Copyright © Glencoe/McGraw-Hill, a division of The McGraw-Hill Companies, Inc.

6-6 Enrichment

Geometric Sequences

A geometric sequence is one in which the ratio between the two terms is constant.

1. **SQUARE NUMBERS** A square number can be modeled by using an area model to create an actual square.

   a. Draw the next two terms in the sequence and determine the fourth term.

   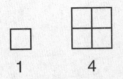

   1   4   9   _____?_____

   b. The function that describes square numbers is n^2. Write this function using multiplication.

   c. Complete the table by finding the missing position and the missing value of the term for square numbers.

Position	3			11	13	15	25
Value of Term	9	64	100			225	625

2. **TRIANGULAR NUMBERS** A triangular number can be modeled by using manipulatives or objects to create triangles. The first three triangular numbers are 1, 3, and 6.

   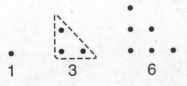

   1   3   6

   a. Draw the next three terms in the sequence in the space above.

   b. What is the ninth term?

   c. The function that describes the triangular number sequence is $n \times \frac{(n + 1)}{2}$. Complete the table by finding either the missing position or missing value of the term for triangular numbers.

Position	3		8	10	15	20	100
Value of Term	6	10			120	210	

6-6 Spreadsheet Activity

Sequences

You can use a spreadsheet to find the pattern in a sequence of numbers and to find the next two numbers in the sequence.

Example Use a spreadsheet to describe the pattern and find the next two terms in the sequence 22, 19, 16, 13, ...

Use the first row of the spreadsheet to enter the data. Enter the numbers using the formula bar. Click on a cell of the spreadsheet, type the number and press **TAB**.

Find the pattern of the sequence in the cell after the last number of the sequence. Since each term is decreased by the same amount, enter an equals sign followed by **D1−C1**. Then press **ENTER**. This returns a value of −3. Each term is 3 less than the term before it.

Find the next two terms in the sequence in the two cells next to the −3. Enter the formula **=D1+E1**. Then press **ENTER**. This returns the value of 10. Repeat this process to find the next term. Enter **=F1+E1**. This returns a value of 7. So, the next two terms in the sequence are 10 and 7.

◇	A	B	C	D	E	F	G	H
1	22	19	16	13	−3	10	7	
2								
3								

Sheet 1 / Sheet 2 / Sheet 3

Exercises

Use a spreadsheet to describe the pattern in each sequence. Then find the next two terms.

1. −6, −4, −2, 0, …

2. 2.5, 5, 7.5, 10, …

3. $\frac{1}{2}, \frac{1}{4}, 0, -\frac{1}{4}, …$

4. 12, 14, 16, 18, …

5. 5.5, 2.5, −0.5, −3.5, …

6. 1.2, 6.2, 11.2, 16.2, …

7. 2.1, 4.3, 6.5, 8.7, …

8. −4.4, −6.1, −7.8, −9.5, …

6-7 Lesson Reading Guide

Proportions and Equations

Get Ready for the Lesson

Read the introduction at the top of page 349 in your textbook. Write your answers below.

1. Write a sentence that describes the relationship between the number of hours she babysits and her earnings.

2. Is the relationship proportional? Explain.

3. What is the rule to find the amount Carli earns for babysitting h hours?

4. If e represents the amount Carli earns, what equation can you use to represent this situation?

Read the Lesson

5. What is the difference between an input value and an output value of a function?

6. Explain the steps involved in using an equation to represent a function.

Remember What You Learned

7. Work with a partner. Create a function table that can be represented with an equation. Exchange function tables with your partner. For the table you receive from your partner, write an equation to represent the function.

6-7 Study Guide and Intervention

Proportions and Equations

A *function table* displays *input* and *output* values that represent a function. The function displayed in a function table can be represented with an *equation*.

Example 1   Write an equation to represent the function displayed in the table.

Examine how the value of each input and output changes.

Input, x	1	2	3	4	5
Output, y	5	10	15	20	25

As each input increases by 1, the output increases by 5. That is, the constant rate of change is 5.

	+1	+1	+1	+1	
Input, x	1	2	3	4	5
Output, y	5	10	15	20	25
	+5	+5	+5	+5	

So, the equation that represents the function is $y = 5x$.

Example 2   Theo earns $6 an hour mowing lawns for his neighbors. Make a table and write an equation for the total amount t Theo earns for mowing h hours. How much will Theo earn for mowing lawns for 11 hours?

As the number of hours increases by 1, the total earned increases by 6.

So, the equation is $t = 6h$.

Let $h = 11$ to find how much Theo will earn in 11 hours.

$t = 6h$
$t = 6 \times 11$ or $66

Hours, h	Total earned, t
1	$6
2	$12
3	$18
4	$24

+1( )+6
+1( )+6
+1( )+6

Exercises

Write an equation to represent the function displayed in each table.

1.

Input, x	1	2	3	4	5
Output, y	2	4	6	8	10

2.

Input, x	0	1	2	3	4
Output, y	0	6	12	18	24

MUSIC Use the following information for Exercises 3–5.

A music store sells each used CD for $4.

3. Make a table to show the relationship between the number of c used CDs purchased and the total cost t.

4. Write an equation to find t, the total cost in dollars for buying c used CDs.

5. How much will it cost to buy 5 used CDs?

6-7 Skills Practice

Proportions and Equations

Write an equation to represent the function displayed in each table.

1.

Input, x	0	1	2	3	4
Output, y	0	3	6	9	12

2.

Input, x	0	1	2	3	4
Output, y	0	1	2	3	4

3.

Input, x	1	2	3	4	5
Output, y	7	14	21	28	35

4.

Input, x	0	1	2	3	4
Output, y	0	10	20	30	40

5.

Input, x	2	4	6	8	10
Output, y	4	8	12	16	20

6.

Input, x	0	1	2	3	4
Output, y	0	12	24	36	48

7.

Input, x	0	1	2	3	4
Output, y	0	8	16	24	32

8.

Input, x	0	1	2	3	4
Output, y	0	20	40	60	80

ANIMALS Use the following information for Exercises 9–11.

A manatee eats an average of 70 pounds of wet vegetation each day.

9. Make a table to show the relationship between the number of p pounds of wet vegetation a manatee eats in d days.

10. Write an equation to find p, the number of pounds of wet vegetation a manatee eats in d days.

11. How many pounds of wet vegetation does a manatee eat in 7 days?

Lesson 6–7

6-7 Practice

Proportions and Equations

Write an equation to represent the function displayed in each table.

1.

Input, x	1	2	3	4	5
Output, y	7	14	21	28	35

2.

Input, x	0	1	2	3	4
Output, y	0	9	18	27	36

3.

Input, x	1	2	3	4	5
Output, y	13	26	39	52	65

4.

Input, x	10	20	30	40	50
Output, y	1	2	3	4	5

5.

Input, x	0	1	2	3	4
Output, y	0	14	28	42	56

6.

Input, x	4	8	12	16	20
Output, y	1	2	3	4	5

7.

Input, x	12	24	36	48	60
Output, y	1	2	3	4	5

8.

Input, x	6	12	18	24	30
Output, y	1	2	3	4	5

BATS Use the following information for Exercises 9–11.

A Little Brown Myotis bat can eat 500 mosquitoes in an hour.

9. In the space at the right, make a table to show the the relationship between the number of hours h and the number of mosquitoes eaten m.

10. Write an equation to find m, the number of mosquitoes a bat eats in h hours.

11. How many mosquitoes can a Little Brown Myotis bat eat in 7 hours?

12. **RECREATION** A community center charges the amount shown in the table for using specialized exercise equipment. Write a sentence and an equation to describe the data. How much will it cost to use the exercise equipment for 6 months?

Number of Months, m	Cost, c
1	$20
2	$40
3	$60

6-7 Word Problem Practice

Proportions and Equations

FITNESS For Exercises 1–3, use the following information.

Rosalia burns 250 Calories for each hour she does aerobics.

1. Make a table to show the relationship between the number of Calories c Rosalia burns doing aerobics for h hours.

2. Write an equation to find c, the number of Calories Rosalia burns in h hours.

3. If Rosalia goes to a 1-hour aerobic class 3 times a week, how many Calories will she burn each week doing aerobics?

4. MUSICALS The table below shows the admission price to the school musical. Write a sentence and an equation to describe the data.

Number of People, n	Total Admission, t
1	$6
2	$12
3	$18

5. MUSICALS In Exercise 4, how much will it cost for a family of 5 to attend the musical?

6. VIDEO GAMES The table below shows the number of points earned for catching bugs in a video game. Write a sentence and an equation to describe the data.

Number of Bugs Caught, b	Total Points, t
1	25
2	50
3	75

6-7 Enrichment

Enchanted Rock

Enchanted Rock is a pink granite dome located in Enchanted Rock State Natural Area in Central Texas. It is of the largest batholiths in the United States. A batholith is made of igneous rock and is the result of volcanic activity. The Enchanted Rock dome rises 425 feet above the ground and is 1825 feet above sea level.

The entrance fee to Enchanted Rock State Natural Area is $5.00 per person.

1. Complete the table to find the entrance cost for groups of different sizes.

Input, x	1	2	3	4	5	6	7	8
Output, y	$5.00	$10.00						

2. Write an equation to represent the function displayed in the table.

3. If the park has 290 visitors, how much money did they collect in entrance fees?

4. A local environmental group is planning to hike up Enchanted Rock. The group will cover each member's entrance fee and will provide lunch for its members. The group budgets $75.00 for lunch, regardless of the number of people on the hike. Complete the table to show the total expenses of the group based on the number of people on the hike.

Input, x	5	10	15	20	25	30
Output, y	$100.00	$125.00				

5. Write an equation to represent the function displayed in the table.

6. The group will hike up the dome at a rate of 1500 feet per hour. What is their hiking speed per minute?

7. Complete the table to show the progression of their hike.

Input (min), x	1	3	5	8	10	12	15	
Output (feet), y	25	75						425

8. Write an equation that represents the function displayed in the table.

9. At the rate given, how long will it take the group to reach the top of Enchanted Rock?

6 Student Recording Sheet

Use this recording sheet with pages 360–361 of the Student Edition.

Part 1: Multiple Choice

Read each question. Then fill in the correct answer.

1. Ⓐ Ⓑ Ⓒ Ⓓ

2. Ⓕ Ⓖ Ⓗ Ⓘ

3. Ⓐ Ⓑ Ⓒ Ⓓ

4. Ⓕ Ⓖ Ⓗ Ⓘ

5. Ⓐ Ⓑ Ⓒ Ⓓ

6. Ⓕ Ⓖ Ⓗ Ⓘ

7. Ⓐ Ⓑ Ⓒ Ⓓ

8. Ⓕ Ⓖ Ⓗ Ⓘ

9. Ⓐ Ⓑ Ⓒ Ⓓ

Part 2: Short Response/Grid in

Record your answer in the blank.

For grid in questions, also enter your answer in the grid by writing each number or symbol in a box. Then fill in the corresponding circle for that number or symbol.

10. _____

11. _____ (*grid in*)

12. _____ (*grid in*)

11.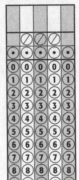

12.

Part 3: Extended Response

Record your answers for Question 13 on the back of this paper.

Assessment

Scoring Rubric for Extended-Response SCORE ____

(Use to score the Extended-Response question on page 361 of the Student Edition.)

General Scoring Guidelines

- If a student gives only a correct numerical answer to a problem but does not show how he or she arrived at the answer, the student will be awarded only 1 credit. All extended response questions require the student to show work.

- A fully correct answer for a multiple-part question requires correct responses for all parts of the question. For example, if a question has three parts, the correct response to one or two parts of the question that required work to be shown is *not* considered a fully correct response.

- Students who use trial and error to solve a problem must show their method. Merely showing that the answer checks or is correct is not considered a complete response for full credit.

Exercise 13 Rubric

Score	Specific Criteria
4	A proportion equivalent to $\frac{45}{90} = \frac{120}{x}$ is written. The proportion is correctly solved to determine that it would take 4 hours to sort 120 books. Another proportion is used to determine that if the rate slowed to 30 books in 90 minutes, it would take 6 hours to sort 120 books.
3	The proportions are correct, but one computational error is made in solving one of the proportions. **OR** One of the proportions and its solution are correct. The other proportion is incorrect, but the solution of the given proportion is correct.
2	One of the proportions and its solution are correct, but the other proportion and its solution are incorrect. **OR** Both of the proportions are correct, but the solutions are incorrect.
1	Only one of the proportions is correct, and neither solution is correct. **OR** One or both of the solutions are correct, but the proportions are not given.
0	Response is completely incorrect.

6 Chapter 6 Quiz 1

(Lessons 6-1 and 6-2)

Write each ratio as a fraction in simplest form. Then explain its meaning.

1.

cats to dogs

1. _____

2.

dimes: quarters

2. _____

3. **BAND** There are 16 girls and 20 boys in the school band. What is the ratio in simplest form of girls to boys?

3. _____

4. **MONEY** Dawson earns $7 per day for watching the neighbor's cat. How much does he earn for watching the cat 3 days?

Amount Earned	7		■
Number of Days	1		3

4. _____

5. **FRUIT** Chin bought 12 pounds of apples for $6. At this rate, how much will it cost to buy 3 pounds of apples?

Pounds of Apples	12		3
Number of Days	6		■

5. _____

- -

6 Chapter 6 Quiz 2

(Lessons 6-3 and 6-4)

Determine if the quantities in each pair of ratios or rates are proportional. Explain your reasoning and express each proportional relationship as a proportion.

1. 180 calories in 3 servings; 350 calories in 5 servings

1. _____

2. 3 hours worked for $15; 7 hours worked for $35

2. _____

Solve each proportion.

3. $\frac{4}{5} = \frac{20}{x}$

4. $\frac{a}{6} = \frac{24}{36}$

3. _____

4. _____

5. If one out of 8 students has a cat, predict how many have a cat in a school of 400 students.

5. _____

Assessment

6 Chapter 6 Quiz 3

(Lessons 6-5 and 6-6)

Use words and symbols to describe the value of each term as a function of its position. Then find the twelfth term in each sequence.

1.

Position	1	2	3	4	n
Value of Term	3	6	9	12	■

1._____

2.

Position	5	6	7	8	n
Value of Term	0	1	2	3	■

2._____

3.

Position	2	3	4	5	n
Value of Term	14	21	28	35	■

3._____

4. **MULTIPLE CHOICE** Which expression was used to create the table at the right?

Position	Value of Term
1	1
2	3
3	5
n	■

A. $2n$ **C.** $n - 1$

B. $3n - 2$ **D.** $2n - 1$

4._____

5. **NUMBER SENSE** Describe the pattern below. Then find the missing number.

54, ■, 42, 36

5._____

- -

6 Chapter 6 Quiz 4

(Lesson 6-7)

Write an equation to represent the function displayed in each table.

1.

Input, x	1	2	3	4
Output, y	4	8	12	16

2.

Input, x	0	1	2	3
Output, y	0	12	24	36

1._____

2._____

SPORTS Use the following information for Questions 3–5.

In a football game, each team earns 6 points for each touchdown they score.

3. Make a table to show the relationship between the number of touchdowns scored t and the total points p.

3.

4. Write an equation to find p, the total points for scoring t touchdowns.

4._____

5. How many points will a team earn if they score 7 touchdowns?

5._____

SCORE _____

6 Chapter 6 Mid-Chapter Test

(Lessons 6-1 through 6-4)

PART I

Write the letter for the correct answer in the blank at the right of each question.

1. Write the ratio *45 boys out of 60 students* as a fraction in simplest form.

   A. $\frac{4}{3}$ B. $\frac{3}{4}$ C. $\frac{3}{7}$ D. $\frac{45}{60}$ 1. _____

2. Write the ratio *420 miles on 15 gallons of gas* as a unit rate.

   F. 28 miles   G. $\frac{1 \text{ mile}}{28 \text{ gallons}}$ H. $\frac{28 \text{ miles}}{1 \text{ gallon}}$ J. $\frac{28 \text{ gallons}}{1 \text{ mile}}$ 2. _____

3. **MONEY** Tia earns $5 per hour baby-sitting. How much does she earn baby-sitting for 4 hours?

Amount Earned	5			■
Number of Hours	1			4

   A. $15   B. $16   C. $18   D. $20   3. _____

For Questions 4 and 5, solve each proportion.

4. $\frac{m}{80} = \frac{15}{20}$

   F. 1,200   G. 60   H. 6   J. $\frac{1}{60}$ 4. _____

5. $\frac{18}{54} = \frac{6}{x}$

   A. 24   B. 20   C. 18   D. 6   5. _____

PART II

Determine if the quantities in each pair of ratios or rates are proportional. Explain your reasoning and express each proportional relationship as a proportion.

6. _____

6. $4 for 12 bagels; $10 for 36 bagels.

7. 110 words typed in 2 minutes; 300 words typed in 6 minutes

   7. _____

8. 135 points in 3 games; 315 points in 7 games

   8. _____

For Questions 9 and 10, solve each proportion.

9. $\frac{5}{m} = \frac{50}{100}$

   9. _____

10. $\frac{27}{36} = \frac{x}{12}$

    10. _____

6 Chapter 6 Vocabulary Test

arithmetic sequence	rate	sequence
equivalent ratio	ratio	term
proportion	ratio table	unit rate
proportional	scaling	

Choose the correct term to complete each sentence.

1. A proportion is a(n) (equation, table) stating that two ratios or rates are equivalent.

   1. _____

2. Each number in a sequence is called a (unit rate, term) of the sequence.

   2. _____

3. (Arithmetic, Equivalent) ratios express the same relationship between two quantities.

   3. _____

4. A (ratio, sequence) is a list of numbers in a specific order.

   4. _____

5. Two quantities are proportional if they have a (different, constant) ratio or rate.

   5. _____

6. In an arithmetic sequence, each term is found by (adding, multiplying) the same number to the previous term.

   6. _____

7. The rate for one unit of a given quantity is called a (proportion, unit rate).

   7. _____

8. Multiplying or dividing two related quantities by the same number is called (equalizing, scaling).

   8. _____

9. In a ratio table, the columns are filled with pairs of numbers that have (different, the same) ratios.

   9. _____

In your own words, define the term.

10. ratio

   10. _____

6 **Chapter 6 Test, Form 1**

Write the letter for the correct answer in the blank at the right of each question.

Write each ratio as a fraction in simplest form.

1. 20 out of 35 people

   A. $\frac{20}{35}$ **B.** $\frac{35}{20}$ **C.** $\frac{8}{14}$ **D.** $\frac{4}{7}$ 1. _____

2. 6 DVDs to 4 tapes

   F. $\frac{3}{2}$ **G.** $\frac{2}{3}$ **H.** $\frac{6}{4}$ **J.** $\frac{4}{6}$ 2. _____

Write each ratio as a unit rate.

3. 6 miles in 2 hours

   A. 3 miles   **C.** $\frac{1}{3}$ mile

   B. 3 miles per hour   **D.** $\frac{1}{3}$ mile per hour   3. _____

4. $2.40 for a dozen pencils

   F. $2.40 per dozen pencils   **H.** $0.20 per pencil

   G. $20 per pencil   **J.** $2 per pencil   4. _____

TICKETS Use the following information for Question 5 and 6.

Rashida bough 3 tickets to a concert for $75.

Number of Tickets	3			5
Money Spent ($)	75			■

5. How much will it cost for 5 tickets to the concert?

   A. $100   **B.** $125   **C.** $150   **D.** $75   5. _____

6. If Rashida spent $100 on tickets, how many tickets did she buy?

   F. 4   **G.** 5   **H.** 6   **J.** 7   6. _____

Solve each proportion.

7. $\frac{m}{32} = \frac{6}{8}$

   A. 192   **B.** 48   **C.** 24   **D.** 43.7   7. _____

8. $\frac{3}{2} = \frac{21}{y}$

   F. 7   **G.** 31.5   **H.** 63   **J.** 14   8. _____

6 Chapter 6 Test, Form 1   (continued)

9. **EXERCISE** The table shows the number of miles Chantel runs each week while training for a marathon. If the pattern continues, how many miles will she run week 5?

Week	1	2	3	4	5
Distance Ran(miles)	3	6	9	12	■

A. 13 **B.** 15 **C.** 18 **D.** 20 9. _____

Use the table below for Questions 10–12.

Position	1	2	3	4	n
Value of Term	2	4	6	8	■

10. Use words to describe the value of each term as a function of its position.

F. multiply by 2 **H.** subtract 2

G. add 2 **J.** divide by 2 10. _____

11. Use symbols to describe the value of each tern as a function of its position.

A. $\frac{2}{n}$ **B.** $n + 2$ **C.** $2n$ **D.** $n - 2$ 11. _____

12. Find the value of the twelfth term in the sequence.

F. 10 **G.** 12 **H.** 16 **J.** 24 12. _____

For Questions 13 and 14, write an equation to represent the function displayed in each table.

13.

Input, x	1	2	3	4	5
Output, y	4	8	12	16	20

A. $y = 5x$ **B.** $y = 4x$ **C.** $y = \frac{x}{4}$ **D.** $y = \frac{x}{5}$ 13. _____

14.

Input, x	1	2	3	4	5
Output, y	2	4	6	8	10

F. $y = 2x$ **G.** $y = 3x$ **H.** $y = \frac{2}{x}$ **J.** $y = \frac{x}{3}$ 14. _____

Bonus Determine if the quantities in the following ratio are proportional. Explain. If so, express the relationship as a proportion.

200 feet to 20 inches; 350 feet to 35 inches **B:** _____

6 **Chapter 6 Test, Form 2A**

SCORE _____

Write the letter for the correct answer in the blank at the right of each question.

Write each ratio as a fraction in simplest form.

1. 42 girls out of 56 people

   A. $\frac{4}{3}$ **B.** $\frac{42}{56}$ **C.** $\frac{6}{8}$ **D.** $\frac{3}{4}$ 1. _____

2. 15 apples to 10 oranges

   F. $\frac{2}{3}$ **G.** $\frac{3}{2}$ **H.** $\frac{15}{10}$ **J.** $\frac{10}{15}$ 2. _____

Write each rate as a unit rate.

3. 350 kilometers in 5 hours

   A. 70 kilometers   **B.** $\frac{70 \text{ kilometers}}{1 \text{ hour}}$ **C.** $\frac{\frac{1}{7} \text{ kilometer}}{1 \text{ hour}}$ **D.** $\frac{350 \text{ kilometers}}{5 \text{ hours}}$ 3. _____

4. $80 for 10 tickets

   F. $\frac{\$80}{10 \text{ tickets}}$ **G.** 8 tickets   **H.** $\frac{\$8}{1 \text{ ticket}}$ **J.** $\frac{8 \text{ tickets}}{\$1}$ 4. _____

MONEY Use the following information for Questions 5 and 6.

Nicholas bought 5 pens for $3.

Number of Pens	5	10
Money Spent ($)	3	■

5. How much will he spend on 10 pens?

   A. $1.50   **B.** $4   **C.** $6   **D.** $9   5. _____

6. If Nicholas spent $9, how many pens did he buy?

   F. 10   **G.** 15   **H.** 20   **J.** 25   6. _____

Solve each proportion.

7. $\frac{18}{27} = \frac{x}{9}$

   A. 6   **B.** 8   **C.** 9   **D.** 36   7. _____

8. $\frac{28}{y} = \frac{4}{7}$

   F. 16   **G.** 50   **H.** 49   **J.** 196   8. _____

Assessment

6 Chapter 6 Test, Form 2A (continued)

9. **NUMBER SENSE** Find the missing number in the pattern below.

2, ■, 28, 41, 54

A. 13   **B.** 15   **C.** 22   **D.** 26   9. _____

Use the table below for Questions 10–12.

Position	5	6	7	8	n
Value of Term	1	2	3	4	■

10. Use words to describe the value of each term as a function of its position.

F. subtract 5   **H.** subtract 4

G. add 1   **J.** divide by 5   10. _____

11. Use symbols to describe the value of each tern as a function of its position.

A. $\frac{n}{5}$ **B.** $n + 5$ **C.** $5n$ **D.** $n - 4$ 11. _____

12. Find the value of the fifteenth term in the sequence.

F. 11   **G.** 12   **H.** 16   **J.** 24   12. _____

For Questions 13 and 14, write an equation to represent the function displayed in each table.

13.

Input, x	1	2	3	4	5
Output, y	6	12	18	24	30

A. $y = x$ **B.** $y = 3x$ **C.** $y = 6x$ **D.** $y = \frac{x}{3}$ 13. _____

14.

Input, x	1	2	3	4	5
Output, y	10	20	30	40	50

F. $y = 10x$ **G.** $y = \frac{x}{10}$ **H.** $y = x + 10$ **J.** $y = 12x$ 14. _____

Bonus Determine if the quantities in the following ratio are proportional. Explain. If so, express the relationship as a proportion.

12 boys to 18 girls; 20 boys to 34 girls   **B:** _____

6 **Chapter 6 Test, Form 2B**

Write the letter for the correct answer in the blank at the right of each question.
Write each ratio as a fraction in simplest form.

1. 64 red cars out of 80 cars

   A. $\frac{64}{80}$ **B.** $\frac{80}{64}$ **C.** $\frac{5}{4}$ **D.** $\frac{4}{5}$ **1.** _____

2. 16 pens to 12 brushes

   F. $\frac{16}{12}$ **G.** $\frac{4}{3}$ **H.** $\frac{12}{16}$ **J.** $\frac{3}{4}$ **2.** _____

Write each rate as a unit rate.

3. 180 miles on 10 gallons

   A. 1.8 miles   **B.** $\frac{18 \text{ miles}}{1 \text{ gallon}}$ **C.** $\frac{\frac{1}{18} \text{ mile}}{1 \text{ gallon}}$ **D.** $\frac{180 \text{ miles}}{10 \text{ gallons}}$ **3.** _____

4. $120 for 12 calculators

   F. $\frac{\$10}{1 \text{ calculator}}$ **G.** $\frac{10 \text{ calculators}}{\$12}$ **H.** $\frac{\$120}{12 \text{ calculators}}$ **J.** 10 calculators   **4.** _____

MONEY Use the following information for Questions 5 and 6.

Angelina bought 6 headbands for $2.

Number of Headbands	6	12
Money Spent ($)	2	■

5. How much will she spend on 12 headbands?

   A. $3   **B.** $4   **C.** $6   **D.** $8   **5.** _____

6. If Angelina spent $8, how many headbands did she buy?

   F. 4   **G.** 12   **H.** 16   **J.** 24   **6.** _____

Solve each proportion.

7. $\frac{m}{8} = \frac{15}{24}$

   A. 5   **B.** 6   **C.** 10   **D.** 15   **7.** _____

8. $\frac{30}{54} = \frac{10}{x}$

   F. 18   **G.** 20   **H.** 23   **J.** 27   **8.** _____

Assessment

9. **NUMBER SENSE** Find the missing number in the pattern below.

63, ■, 49, 42, 35

A. 29   B. 51   C. 56   D. 70   9. _____

Use the table below for Questions 10–12.

Position	1	2	3	4	n
Value of Term	8	9	10	11	■

10. Use words to describe the value of each term as a function of its position.

F. add 7   H. subtract 7

G. multiply by 7   J. divide by 7   10. _____

11. Use symbols to describe the value of each term as a function of its position.

A. $\frac{n}{7}$ B. $n + 7$ C. $7n$ D. $n - 7$ 11 _____

12. Find the value of the fifteenth term in the sequence.

F. 19   G. 22   H. 24   J. 37   12. _____

For Questions 13 and 14, write an equation to represent the function displayed in each table.

13.
Input, x	1	2	3	4	5
Output, y	3	6	9	12	15

A. $y = x$ B. $y = 3x$ C. $y = 6x$ D. $y = \frac{x}{3}$ 13. _____

14.
Input, x	1	2	3	4	5
Output, y	12	24	36	48	60

F. $y = x + 11$ G. $y = \frac{x}{12}$ H. $y = 12x$ J. $y = 14x$ 14. _____

Bonus Determine if the quantities in the following ratio are proportional. Explain. If so, express the relationship as a proportion.

10 baseball cards to 18 football cards; 15 baseball cards to 27 football cards

B: _____

6 **Chapter 6 Test, Form 2C**

Write each ratio as a fraction in simplest form.

1. 16 blue-eyed people out of 50 people

1. _____

2. 18 rectangles to 4 circles

2. _____

Write each ratio as a unit rate.

3. 424 kilometers in 8 hours

3. _____

4. $60 for 12 months

4. _____

5. **FOOD** The school cook uses 10 pounds of potatoes to make mashed potatoes for 40 students. How many pounds of potatoes does the school cook need to make mashed potatoes for 120 students?

5. _____

Pounds of Potatoes	10		■
Students Served	40		120

Determine if the quantities in each pair of ratios or rates are proportional. Explain your reasoning and express each proportional relationship as a proportion.

6. 12 miles jogged in 120 minutes; 8 miles jogged in 100 minutes

6. _____

7. 3 hours worked for $18; 5 hours worked for $30

7. _____

Solve each proportion.

8. $\frac{10}{15} = \frac{20}{x}$

8. _____

9. $\frac{9}{m} = \frac{27}{30}$

9. _____

10. $\frac{c}{25} = \frac{16}{200}$

10. _____

Assessment

11. NUMBER SENSE Find the missing number in the pattern below.

11. _____

31, ■ 21, 16, 11

12. GEOMETRY Draw the next figure in the pattern below.

12.

 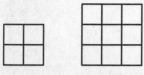

Use the table below for Questions 13–15.

Position	1	2	3	4	n
Value of Term	8	16	24	32	■

13. Use words to describe the value of each term as a function of its position.

13. _____

14. Use symbols to describe the value of each tern as a function of its position.

14. _____

15. Find the value of the fifteenth term in the sequence.

15. _____

For Questions 16–18, write an equation to represent the function displayed in each table.

16.

Input, x	1	2	3	4	5
Output, y	3	6	9	12	15

16. _____

17.

Input, x	0	1	2	3	4
Output, y	0	9	18	27	36

17. _____

18.

Input, x	1	2	3	4	5
Output, y	12	24	36	48	60

18. _____

Bonus EXERCISE Sasha takes 8 breaths per 10 seconds during aerobics. At this rate, about how many breaths would Sasha take in 2 minutes of aerobics?

B: _____

SCORE _____

Write each ratio as a fraction in simplest form.

1. $25 out of every $500 collected

1. _____

2. 12 children to 20 adults

2. _____

Write each ratio as a unit rate.

3. 240 miles on 8 gallons of gasoline

3. _____

4. 180 students for 6 classes

4. _____

5. **FOOD** Maggie's grandmother uses 3 pounds of peaches to make 2 peach pies. How many pounds of peaches does she need to make 6 peach pies?

5. _____

Pounds of Peaches	3	■
Pies	2	6

Determine if the quantities in each pair of ratios or rates are proportional. Explain your reasoning and express each proportional relationship as a proportion.

6. 100 calories burned in 20 minutes; 175 calories burned in 35 minutes

6. _____

7. $24 for 6 hours of work; $36 for 8 hours of work

7. _____

Solve each proportion.

8. $\frac{m}{9} = \frac{30}{27}$

8. _____

9. $\frac{6}{d} = \frac{18}{21}$

9. _____

10. $\frac{14}{16} = \frac{7}{f}$

10. _____

Assessment

11. **NUMBER SENSE** Find the missing number in the pattern below.

    74, ■, 96, 107, 118

11. _____

12. **GEOMETRY** Draw the next figure in the pattern below.

12.

Use the table below for Questions 13–15.

Position	9	10	11	12	n
Value of Term	3	4	5	6	■

13. Use words to describe the value of each term as a function of its position.

13. _____

14. Use symbols to describe the value of each tern as a function of its position.

14. _____

15. Find the value of the sixteenth term in the sequence.

15. _____

For Questions 16–18, write an equation to represent the function displayed in each table.

16.

Input, x	1	2	3	4	5
Output, y	4	8	12	16	20

16. _____

17.

Input, x	0	1	2	3	4
Output, y	0	8	16	24	32

17. _____

18.

Input, x	1	2	3	4	5
Output, y	11	22	33	44	55

18. _____

Bonus EXERCISE Reese takes 6 breaths per 10 seconds while she is jogging. At this rate, about how many breaths would Reese take in 3 minutes of jogging?

B: _____

6 | Chapter 6 Test, Form 3

Write each ratio as a fraction in simplest form.

1. 60 fish to 440 frogs

2. 35 shots made out of 55 attempted

Write each ratio as a unit rate.

3. 162 heartbeats in 60 seconds

4. 135 push-ups in 6 minutes

5. **MONEY** Lamar earns an allowance of $4 each week. How much does he earn every 4 weeks?

Allowance	4		■
Number of Weeks	1		4

6. **FIELD TRIP** There must by 1 adult for every 9 students going to the art museum. If there are 54 students in the sixth grade going on the field trip, how many adults must attend?

Number of Adults	1				■
Number of Students	9				54

Determine if the quantities in each pair of ratios or rates are proportional. Explain your reasoning and express each proportional relationship as a proportion.

7. $3 for 10 folders; $6 for 24 folders

8. $168 raised for washing 24 cars; $280 raised for washing 40 cars

Solve each proportion.

9. $\frac{z}{14} = \frac{48}{168}$

10. $\frac{60}{y} = \frac{180}{120}$

11. $\frac{64}{16} = \frac{b}{4}$

1. _____

2. _____

3. _____

4. _____

5. _____

6. _____

7. _____

8. _____

9. _____

10. _____

11. _____

Assessment

6 Chapter 6 Test, Form 3 *(continued)*

12. **NUMBER SENSE** Find the missing number in the pattern below.

    8, ■, 72, 216, 648

    12. _____

13. **MONEY** In 2002, Lindsay earned $21,500 per year, and Rondell earned $23,000 per year. Each year, Rondell received a $1,000 raise, and Lindsay received a $1,500 raise. In what year will they earn the same amount of money? How much will it be?

    13. _____

Use the table below for Questions 14–16.

Position	1	2	3	4	n
Value of Term	9	18	27	36	■

14. Use words to describe the value of each term as a function of its position.

    14. _____

15. Use symbols to describe the value of each tern as a function of its position.

    15. _____

16. Find the value of the sixteenth term in the sequence.

    16. _____

17. **DVDS** Carlos spent $36 on 4 DVDs. At this rate, how much would 7 DVDs cost?

    17. _____

For Questions 18–20, write an equation to represent the function displayed in each table.

18.

Input, x	1	2	3	4	5
Output, y	5	10	15	20	25

    18. _____

19.

Input, x	0	1	2	3	4
Output, y	0	7	14	21	28

    19. _____

20.

Input, x	1	2	3	4	5
Output, y	14	28	42	56	70

    20. _____

Bonus What expression was used to create the table at the right?

Position	Value of Term
1	5
2	7
3	9
n	■

    B: _____

6 Chapter 6 Extended-Response Test

Demonstrate your knowledge by giving a clear, concise solution to each problem. Be sure to include all relevant drawings and justify your answers. You may show your solution in more than one way or investigate beyond the requirements of the problem. If necessary, record your answer on another piece of paper.

1. **a.** Tell in your own words the meaning of *ratio*.

   b. Give an example of a ratio. Write the ratio in four ways.

   c. Tell in your own words the meanings of *rate* and *unit rate*. Give an example of a unit rate and an example of a rate that is not a unit rate.

   d. Tell in your own words the meaning of *proportion*.

   e. Write a word problem that uses a proportion.

   f. Solve the word problem in part **e**. Explain each step.

2. **TICKETS** The table below shows the cost of tickets to a county fair.

Number of Tickets	1	2	3	4	5
Total Cost ($)	7	14	21	28	35

   a. Use words to describe the total cost of tickets to the fair as a function of the number of tickets purchased.

   b. Use symbols to describe the total cost of tickets to the fair as a function of the number of tickets purchased.

   c. Write an equation to represent the function displayed in the table. Define the variables.

   d. How much will it cost a family to buy 7 tickets?

   e. If the sixth grade class took a field trip to the fair and spent $420 on tickets, how many tickets did they buy?

Assessment

6 Standardized Test Practice

(Chapters 1–6)

Part 1: Multiple Choice

Instructions: Fill in the appropriate circle for the best answer.

1. Write $10 \times 10 \times 10 \times 10$ using an exponent. Then find the value of the power. (Lesson 1-3)

   A $4 \times 10; 40$ **C** $10^4; 10{,}000$

   B $10^4; 1{,}000$ **D** $10 \times 4; 10{,}000$ 1. Ⓐ Ⓑ Ⓒ Ⓓ

2. Find the value of $24 \div 4 + 3 \times (2 + 7)$. (Lesson 1-4)

   F 81   **G** 33   **H** 25   **J** 19   2. Ⓕ Ⓖ Ⓗ Ⓙ

3. Which data set has a mean of 12 and a median of 14? (Lessons 2-6 and 2-7)

   A {13, 12, 11} **B** {10, 12, 20} **C** {3, 14, 20} **D** {12, 4, 16, 16}   3. Ⓐ Ⓑ Ⓒ Ⓓ

4. Estimate $4.52 + 3.699 + 4.1754 + 4$ using clustering. (Lesson 3-4)

   F 10   **G** 12   **H** 16   **J** 20   4. Ⓕ Ⓖ Ⓗ Ⓙ

5. **MONEY** Jenny earned \$18, \$24, and \$27 for babysitting for three days. She only charges for whole hours. What is the minimum she charges per hour? (Lesson 4-1)

   A \$18   **B** \$6   **C** \$3   **D** \$2   5. Ⓐ Ⓑ Ⓒ Ⓓ

6. Which fraction is less than $\frac{4}{9}$? (Lesson 4-6)

   F $\frac{3}{5}$ **G** $\frac{1}{2}$ **H** $\frac{5}{11}$ **J** $\frac{3}{7}$ 6. Ⓕ Ⓖ Ⓗ Ⓙ

7. Add $\frac{5}{9} + \frac{5}{12}$. (Lesson 5-3)

   A $\frac{10}{21}$ **B** $\frac{5}{6}$ **C** $\frac{35}{36}$ **D** $\frac{7}{9}$ 7. Ⓐ Ⓑ Ⓒ Ⓓ

8. **MUSIC** Amita owns an electric guitar that is $3\frac{1}{12}$ feet long. Rishi owns a Spanish guitar that is $2\frac{1}{4}$ feet long. How much longer is Amita's guitar than Rishi's? (Lesson 1-3)

   F $\frac{1}{6}$ foot   **G** $\frac{5}{12}$ foot   **H** $\frac{3}{4}$ foot   **J** $\frac{5}{6}$ foot   8. Ⓕ Ⓖ Ⓗ Ⓙ

9. **SOCCER** There are 18 boys and 24 girls playing spring soccer. What is the ratio in simplest form of boys to girls? (Lesson 4-1)

   A $\frac{18}{24}$ **B** $\frac{9}{12}$ **C** $\frac{3}{4}$ **D** $\frac{3}{5}$ 9. Ⓐ Ⓑ Ⓒ Ⓓ

6 Standardized Test Practice *(continued)*

(Chapters 1–6)

10. **MONEY** Joaquin spent $4 on 6 packs of baseball cards. How much will he spend on 12 packs of baseball cards? (Lesson 6-2)

Packs of Baseball Cards	6	12
Money Spent ($)	4	■

   F $6   **G** $7   **H** $8   **J** $12   10. Ⓕ Ⓖ Ⓗ Ⓙ

11. Solve the proportion $\frac{7}{8} = \frac{x}{32}$. (Lesson 6-4)

   A 14   **B** 21   **C** 26   **D** 28   11. Ⓐ Ⓑ Ⓒ Ⓓ

Use the table for Questions 12 and 13.

Position	1	2	3	4	n
Value of Term	7	8	9	10	■

12. What symbols describe the value of each term as a function of its position? (Lesson 6-6)

   F $6 + n$ **G** $6 - n$ **H** $6n$ **J** $6 \div n$ 12. Ⓕ Ⓖ Ⓗ Ⓙ

13. Find the value of the fourteenth term in the sequence. (Lesson 6-6)

   A 8   **B** 14   **C** 20   **D** 84   13. Ⓐ Ⓑ Ⓒ Ⓓ

14. Which equation represents the function displayed in the table? (Lesson 6-7)

Input, x	1	2	3	4	5
Output, y	5	10	15	20	25

   F $y = 5x$ **G** $y = 5 + x$ **H** $y = 10x$ **J** $y = 10 + x$ 14. Ⓕ Ⓖ Ⓗ Ⓙ

Part 2: Short Response

Instructions: Write your answers to each question in the space provided.

15. Find $353.18 - 143.27$. (Lesson 3-5)   15. _____

16. Solve the proportion $\frac{x}{45} = \frac{5}{9}$. (Lesson 6-4)   16. _____

Assessment

6 Standardized Test Practice (continued)
(Chapters 1–6)

17. Find the prime factorization of 66. (Lesson 1-2)

17. _____

18. **BOOKS** The table shows Tanya's book collection. Make a bar graph of the data.. (Lesson 2-2)

Book	Frequency
Poetry	2
Fantasy	6
Mystery	10

18.

Tanya's Books

19. Order 8.4, 2.5, 1.375, 1.5, and 1.44 from least to greatest. (Lesson 3-2)

19. _____

20. Write the ratio 24 bottles of water for $6.00 as a unit rate. (Lesson 6-1)

20. _____

21. Determine if the quantities in the following ratio are proportional. Explain. If so, express the relationship as a proportion. (Lesson 6-3)

21. _____

15 miles biked in 80 minuts; 60 miles biked in 320 minutes

22. Use the sequence displayed in the table below.

Position	6	7	8	9	n
Value of Term	2	3	4	5	■

a. Use words to describe the value of each term as a function of its position. (Lesson 6-6)

22a. _____

b. Use symbols to describe the value of each term as a function of its position. (Lesson 6-6)

22b. _____

c. Find the value of the sixteenth term in the sequence. (Lesson 6-6)

22c. _____

d. Write an equation to represent the function displayed in the table. Let n represent the position, and let v represent the value of the term. (Lesson 6-7)

22d. _____

Lesson 6-1

NAME _____ DATE _____ PERIOD _____

6-1 Lesson Reading Guide

Ratios and Rates

Get Ready for the Lesson

Complete the Mini Lab at the top of page 314 in your textbook. Write your answers below.

1. Compare the number of blue paper clips to the number of red paper clips using the word *more* and then using the word *times*. **There are 4 more blue paper clips than red paper clips. There are three times as many blue paper clips than red paper clips.**

2. Compare the number of red paper clips to the number of blue paper clips using the word *less* and then using a fraction. **There are 4 less red paper clips than blue paper clips. The number of red paper clips is $\frac{1}{3}$ the number of blue paper clips.**

Read the Lesson

3. A ratio compares amounts of two different things by division. Tell what different things are compared in the examples in your textbook.

   Example 1 ____ **paper clips**

   Example 2 ____ **favorite flavor of gum**

4. Write the ratio of *2 pens out of a total of 3 pens* 3 different ways.

   $\dfrac{2}{3}$ _____ **2 to 3** _____ **2:3**

5. What is the denominator in a unit rate? **1**

Remember What You Learned

6. Go to your local grocery store and make a list of unit rates that are used to price items in the store. Also, compare prices for different brands of a certain product. How can you find out which brand provides the best value? Does the store help you to make the comparison? If so, how? **See students' work.**

NAME _____ DATE _____ PERIOD _____

Chapter Resources

6 Anticipation Guide

Ratio, Proportion, and Functions

STEP 1 *Before you begin Chapter 6*

- Read each statement.
- Decide whether you Agree (A) or Disagree (D) with the statement.
- Write A or D in the first column OR if you are not sure whether you agree or disagree, write NS (Not Sure).

STEP 1 A, D, or NS	Statement	STEP 2 A or D
	1. A ratio is a comparison of two numbers by division.	A
	2. A ratio can be simplified in the same way as a fraction.	A
	3. A rate is a ratio of two measurements with the same kind of units.	D
	4. An example of a unit rate is $\dfrac{132 \text{ miles}}{2 \text{ hours}}$.	D
	5. $\dfrac{3}{5} = \dfrac{12}{20}$ is an example of a proportion.	A
	6. Cross products can be used to determine if two ratios form a proportion.	A
	7. Looking for patterns in a problem can lead to a solution.	A
	8. A sequence is a list of numbers in order from least to greatest.	D
	9. Each number in a sequence is called a factor of that sequence.	D
	10. The equation $y = 5x$ could represent a sequence in which each output is equal to 5 times the input.	A

STEP 2 *After you complete Chapter 6*

- Reread each statement and complete the last column by entering an A (Agree) or a D (Disagree).
- Did any of your opinions about the statements change from the first column?
- For those statements that you mark with a D, use a separate sheet of paper to explain why you disagree. Use examples, if possible.

Answers

Lesson 6-1

6-1 Skills Practice

Ratios and Rates

Write each ratio as a fraction in simplest form.

1. 3 sailboats to 6 motorboats $\frac{1}{2}$

2. 4 tulips to 9 daffodils $\frac{4}{9}$

3. 5 baseballs to 25 softballs $\frac{1}{5}$

4. 2 days out of 8 days $\frac{1}{4}$

5. 6 poodles out of 18 dogs $\frac{1}{3}$

6. 10 yellow eggs out of 12 colored eggs $\frac{5}{6}$

7. 12 sheets of paper out of 28 $\frac{3}{7}$

8. 18 hours out of 24 hours $\frac{3}{4}$

9. 16 elms out of 20 trees $\frac{4}{5}$

10. 15 trumpets to 9 trombones $\frac{5}{3}$

11. 5 ducks to 30 geese $\frac{1}{6}$

12. 14 lions to 10 tigers $\frac{7}{5}$

13. 6 sodas out of 16 drinks $\frac{3}{8}$

14. 20 blue jays out of 35 birds $\frac{4}{7}$

Write each rate as a unit rate.

15. 14 hours in 2 weeks **7 hours per week**

16. 36 pieces of candy for 6 children **6 pieces of candy per child**

17. 8 teaspoons for 4 cups **2 tsp per cup**

18. 8 tomatoes for $2 **4 tomatoes per dollar**

19. $28 for 4 hours **$7 per hour**

20. 150 miles in 3 hours **50 miles per hour**

21. $18 for 3 CDs **$6 per CD**

22. 48 logs on 6 trucks **8 logs per truck**

23. Write the ratio *21 wins to 9 losses* as a fraction in simplest form. $\frac{7}{3}$

24. Write the ratio *$12 dollars for 3 tickets* as a unit rate. **$4 per ticket**

6-1 Study Guide and Intervention

Ratios and Rates

A **ratio** is a comparison of two numbers by division. A common way to express a ratio is as a fraction in simplest form. Ratios can also be written in other ways. For example, the ratio $\frac{2}{3}$ can be written as 2 to 3, 2 out of 3, or 2:3.

Examples Refer to the diagram at the right.

1 Write the ratio in simplest form that compares the number of circles to the number of triangles.

$\begin{array}{c} \text{circles} \rightarrow \\ \text{triangles} \rightarrow \end{array} \frac{4}{5}$ The GCF of 4 and 5 is 1.

So, the ratio of circles to triangles is $\frac{4}{5}$, 4 to 5, or 4:5.
For every 4 circles, there are 5 triangles.

2 Write the ratio in simplest form that compares the number of circles to the total number of figures.

$\begin{array}{c} \text{circles} \rightarrow \\ \text{total figures} \rightarrow \end{array} \frac{4}{10} = \frac{2}{5}$ The GCF of 4 and 10 is 2.

The ratio of circles to the total number of figures is $\frac{2}{5}$, 2 to 5, or 2:5.
For every two circles, there are five total figures.

A **rate** is a ratio of two measurements having different kinds of units. When a rate is simplified so that it has a denominator of 1, it is called a **unit rate**.

Example 3 Write the ratio *20 students to 5 computers* as a unit rate.

$\frac{20 \text{ students}}{5 \text{ computers}} = \frac{4 \text{ students}}{1 \text{ computer}}$ Divide the numerator and the denominator by 5 to get a denominator of 1.

The ratio written as a unit rate is *4 students to 1 computer*.

Exercises

Write each ratio as a fraction in simplest form.

1. 2 guppies out of 6 fish $\frac{1}{3}$
2. 12 puppies to 15 kittens $\frac{4}{5}$
3. 5 boys out of 10 students $\frac{1}{2}$

Write each rate as a unit rate.

4. 6 eggs for 3 people **2 eggs per person**
5. $12 for 4 pounds **$3 per pound**
6. 40 pages in 8 days **5 pages per day**

Lesson 6-1

NAME _____ DATE _____ PERIOD _____

6-1 Word Problem Practice

Ratios and Rates

1. FOOTBALL In a recent the NFL season, the Miami Dolphins won 4 games and the Oakland Raiders won 5 games. What is the ratio of wins for the Dolphins to wins for the Raiders?
$\frac{4}{5}$

2. GARDENING Rod has 10 rosebushes, 2 of which produce yellow roses. Write the ratio *2 yellow rosebushes out of 10 rosebushes* in simplest form.
$\frac{1}{5}$

3. TENNIS Nancy and Lisa played 20 sets of tennis. Nancy won 12 of them. Write the ratio of Nancy's wins to the total number of sets in simplest form.
$\frac{3}{5}$

4. AGES Oscar is 16 years old and his sister Julia is 12 years old. What will be the ratio of Oscar's age to Julia's age in 2 years? Write as a fraction in simplest form.
$\frac{9}{7}$

5. MOVIES Four friends paid a total of $32 for movie tickets. What is the ratio $32 *for 4 people* written as a unit rate?
$8 per person

6. WORKING At a warehouse, the employees can unload 18 trucks in 6 hours. What is the unit rate for unloading trucks? **3 trucks per hour**

7. ANIMALS A reindeer can run 96 miles in 3 hours. At this rate, how far can a reindeer run in 1 hour? Explain.
32 mi; Sample answer: If it takes a reindeer 3 hours to run 96 mi, it must take 3 ÷ 3 = 1 h to run 96 ÷ 3 = 32 mi.

8. SHOPPING Jenny wants to buy cereal that comes in large and small boxes. The 32-ounce box costs $4.16, and the 14-ounce box costs $2.38. Which box is less expensive per ounce? Explain. **The larger box is less expensive. It costs $0.13 per oz, and the smaller box costs $0.17 per oz.**

NAME _____ DATE _____ PERIOD _____

6-1 Practice

Ratios and Rates

1. FRUITS Find the ratio of bananas to oranges in the graphic at the right. Write the ratio as a fraction in simplest form. Then explain its meaning. $\frac{1}{3}$; **This means for every 1 banana, there are 3 oranges.**

2. MODEL TRAINS Hiroshi has 4 engines and 18 box cars. Find the ratio of engines to box cars. Write the ratio as a fraction in simplest form. Then explain its meaning. $\frac{2}{9}$; **This means for every 2 engines, there are 9 box cars.**

3. ZOOS A petting zoo has 5 lambs, 11 rabbits, 4 goats, and 4 piglets. Find the ratio of goats to the total number of animals. Then explain its meaning. $\frac{1}{6}$, **1 to 6, or 1:6; This means 1 out of every 6 animals is a goat.**

4. FOOD At the potluck, there were 6 pecan pies, 7 lemon pies, 13 cherry pies, and 8 apple pies. Find the ratio of apple pies to the total number of pies. Then explain its meaning.
$\frac{4}{17}$, **4 to 17, or 4:17; This means 4 out of every 17 pies were apple pies.**

Write each rate as a unit rate.

5. 3 inches of snow in 6 hours $\frac{0.5 \text{ in.}}{1 \text{ h}}$

6. $46 for 5 toys $\frac{\$9.20}{1 \text{ toy}}$

7. TRAINS The Nozomi train in Japan can travel 558 miles in 3 hours. At this rate, how far can the train travel per hour? **186 mi**

ANALYZE TABLES For Exercises 8 and 9, refer to the table showing tide pool animals.

Animals Found in a Tide Pool	
Animal	Number
Anemones	11
Limpets	14
Snails	18
Starfish	9

8. Find the ratio of limpets to snails. Then explain its meaning.
$\frac{7}{9}$, **7 to 9, or 7:9; This means there are 7 limpets for every 9 snails.**

9. Find the ratio of snails to the total number of animals. Then explain its meaning.
$\frac{9}{26}$, **9 to 26, or 9:26; This means that 9 out of 26 animals are snails.**

Answers

Answers (Lessons 6-1 and 6-2)

6-2 Lesson Reading Guide

Ratio Tables

Get Ready for the Lesson

Read the introduction at the top of page 322 in your textbook. Write your answers below.

1. How many cans of juice and how many cans of water would you need to make 2 batches that have the same taste? 3 batches? Draw a picture to support your answers.

2 pitchers: 2 cans of juice and 6 cans of water;

3 pitchers: 3 cans of juice and 9 cans of water

2. Find the ratio in simplest form of juice to water needed for 1, 2, and 3 batches of juice. What do you notice? **1:3, 1:3, 1:3; The ratios are the same.**

Read the Lesson

3. In a ratio table, what relationship exists between the columns? **The numbers in each column have the same ratio.**

4. Explain how you can check your answers when using a ratio table to solve a problem. **Sample answer: Check to see if the ratio of the new quantities is equivalent to the ratio of the original quantities.**

Remember What You Learned

5. Think of a real-world situation in which you would need to find equivalent ratios. Make a ratio table for this situation. Would you need to *scale back* or *scale forward* in this situation to find equivalent ratios? Explain. **See students' work.**

6-1 Enrichment

Ratios and Rectangles

1. Use a centimeter ruler to measure the width and the length of each rectangle. Then express the ratio of the width to the length as a fraction in simplest form.

A: width = 2 cm
length = 4 cm
ratio = $\frac{1}{2}$

B: width = 3 cm
length = 5 cm
ratio = $\frac{3}{5}$

C: width = 4 cm
length = 6 cm
ratio = $\frac{2}{3}$

D: width = 6 cm
length = 9 cm
ratio = $\frac{2}{3}$

E: width = 4.8 cm
length = 4.8 cm
ratio = $\frac{1}{1}$

2. Similar figures have the same shape, but not necessarily the same size. Two rectangles are similar if the ratio of the width to the length is the same for each. Which rectangles in Exercise 1 are similar? **C and D**

3. For centuries artists and architects have used a shape called the **golden rectangle** because people seem to find it most pleasant to look at. In a golden rectangle, the ratio of the width to the length is a little less than $\frac{5}{8}$. Which rectangle in Exercise 1 is most nearly a golden rectangle? **B**

Lesson 6-2

NAME _____ DATE _____ PERIOD _____

6-2 Study Guide and Intervention

Ratio Tables

A **ratio table** organizes data into columns that are filled with pairs of numbers that have the same ratio, or are equivalent. **Equivalent ratios** express the same relationship between two quantities.

Example 1 BAKING You need 1 cup of rolled oats to make 24 oatmeal cookies. **Use the ratio table at the right to find how many oatmeal cookies you can make with 5 cups of rolled oats.**

Cups of Oats	1	5
Oatmeal Cookies	24	■

Find a pattern and extend it.

Cups of Oats	1	2	3	4	5
Oatmeal Cookies	24	48	72	96	120

(+1 across top; +24 across bottom)

So, 120 oatmeal cookies can be made with 5 cups of rolled oats.

Multiplying or dividing two related quantities by the same number is called **scaling**. You may sometimes need to *scale back* and then *scale forward* or vice versa to find an equivalent ratio.

Example 2 SHOPPING A department store has socks on sale for 4 pairs for $10. Use the ratio table at the right to find the cost of 6 pairs of socks.

Pairs of Socks	4	6
Cost in Dollars	10	■

There is no whole number by which you can multiply 4 to get 6. Instead, scale back to 2 and then forward to 6.

Pairs of Socks	2	4	6
Cost in Dollars	5	10	15

(÷ 2) (× 3)

So, the cost of 6 pairs of socks would be $15.

Exercises

1. EXERCISE Keewan bikes 6 miles in 30 minutes. At this rate, how long would it take him to bike 18 miles? **90 min**

Distance Biked (mi)	6	18
Time (min)	30	■

2. HOBBIES Christine is making fleece blankets. 6 yards of fleece will make 2 blankets. How many blankets can she make with 9 yards of fleece? **3 blankets**

Yards of Fleece	6	9
Number of Blankets	2	■

NAME _____ DATE _____ PERIOD _____

6-2 Skills Practice

Ratio Tables

For Exercises 1–4, use the ratio table given to solve each problem.

1. BAKING A recipe for 1 apple pie calls for 6 cups of sliced apples. How many cups of sliced apples are needed to make 4 apple pies? **24 cups**

Number of Pies	1	4
Cups of Sliced Apples	6	■

2. BASEBALL CARDS Justin bought 40 packs of baseball cards for a discounted price of $64. If he sells 10 packs of baseball cards to a friend at cost, how much should he charge? **$16**

Number of Baseball Card Packs	10	40
Cost in Dollars	■	64

3. SOUP A recipe that yields 12 cups of soup calls for 28 ounces of beef broth. How many ounces of beef broth do you need to make 18 cups of the soup? **42 oz**

Number of Cups	12	18
Ounces of Beef Broth	28	■

4. ANIMALS At a dog shelter, a 24-pound bag of dog food will feed 36 dogs a day. How many dogs would you expect to feed with a 16-pound bag of dog food? **24 dogs**

Pounds of Dog Food	16	24
Number of Dogs Fed	■	36

5. AUTOMOBILES Mr. Fink's economy car can travel 420 miles on a 12-gallon tank of gas. Use a ratio table to determine how many miles he can travel on 8 gallons. **280 mi**

Miles	420	■
Gallons	12	8

Answers

Answers (Lesson 6-2)

Word Problem Practice section

NAME _____ DATE _____ PERIOD _____

6-2 Word Problem Practice

Ratio Tables

For Exercises 1–4, use the ratio tables below.

Table 1

Cups of Flour	1
Number of Cookies	30

Table 2

Number of Books	6
Cost in Dollars	10

1. **BAKING** In Table 1, how many cookies could you make with 4 cups of flour? **120 cookies**

2. **BAKING** In Table 1, how many cups of flour would you need to make 90 cookies? **3 cups**

3. **BOOKS** In Table 2, at this rate how many books can you buy with $5? **3 books**

4. **BOOKS** In Table 2, at this rate, how much would it cost to buy 9 books? **$15**

5. **FRUIT** Patrick buys 12 bunches of bananas for $9 for the after school program. Use a ratio table to determine how much Patrick will pay for 8 bunches of bananas. **$6**

6. **HIKING** On a hiking trip, LaShana notes that she hikes about 12 kilometers every 4 hours. If she continues at this rate, use a ratio table to determine about how many kilometers she could hike in 6 hours. **18 km**

Chapter 6   19   Course 1

Practice section

NAME _____ DATE _____ PERIOD _____

6-2 Practice

Ratio Tables

For Exercises 1–3, use the ratio tables given to solve each problem.

1. **CAMPING** To disinfect 1 quart of stream water to make it drinkable, you need to add 2 tablets of iodine. How many tablets do you need to disinfect 4 quarts? **8 tablets**

Number of Tablets	2	■
Number of Quarts	1	4

2. **BOOKS** A book store bought 160 copies of a book from the publisher for $4,000. If the store gives away 2 books, how much money will it lose? **$50**

Number of Copies	160	2
Cost in Dollars	4,000	■

3. **BIRDS** An ostrich can run at a rate of 50 miles in 60 minutes. At this rate, how long would it take an ostrich to run 18 miles? **21.6 min**

Distance Run (mi)	50	18
Time (min)	60	■

4. **DISTANCE** If 10 miles is about 16 kilometers and the distance between two towns is 45 miles, use a ratio table to find the distance between the towns in kilometers. Explain your reasoning. **72 km; If 10 mi is about 16 km, 90 mi is about 144 km. Since 45 mi is half of 90 mi, or 90 ÷ 2, the distance in km must also be half, or 144 ÷ 2.**

5. **SALARY** Luz earns $400 for 40 hours of work. Use a ratio table to determine how much she earns for 6 hours of work. **$60**

Sample answer:

Salary	400	10	60
Hours	40	1	6

RECIPES For Exercises 6–8, use the following information.

A soup that serves 16 people calls for 2 cans of chopped clams, 4 cups of chicken broth, 6 cups of milk, and 4 cups of cubed potatoes.

6. Create a ratio table to represent this situation.

Sample answer:

People Served	16
Chopped Clams (cans)	2
Chicken Broth (cups)	4
Milk (cups)	6
Cubed Potatoes (cups)	4

7. How much of each ingredient would you need to make an identical recipe that serves 8 people? 32 people?
1 can clams, 2 cups broth, 3 cups milk, 2 cups potatoes; 4 cans clams, 8 cups broth, 12 cups milk, 8 cups potatoes

8. How much of each ingredient would you need to make an identical recipe that serves 24 people? Explain your reasoning.
3 cans clams, 6 cups broth, 9 cups milk, 6 cups potatoes; Since 24 is three times 8, multiply the ingredients for 8 servings by three.

Chapter 6   18   Course 1

NAME _____ DATE _____ PERIOD _____

6-3 Lesson Reading Guide

Proportions

Get Ready for the Lesson

Read the introduction at the top of page 329 in your textbook.
Write your answers below.

1. Express the relationship between the total cost and number of prints he made for each situation as a rate in fraction form.

$\dfrac{\$2}{10\ prints}$; $\dfrac{\$6}{30\ prints}$

2. Compare the relationship between the numerators of each rate you wrote in Exercise 1. Compare the relationship between the denominators of these rates. **Sample answer: The numerator in the second rate is 3 times the numerator in the first rate. The denominator in the second rate is 3 times the denominator in the first rate.**

3. Are the rates you wrote in Exercise 1 equivalent? Explain. **The rates are equivalent since they each have the same unit rate of** $\dfrac{\$1}{5\ prints}$.

Read the Lesson

4. Look at the Key Concept box on page 329. How can you tell that the two examples given are proportions? **Sample answer: The numerator and denominator in the first ratio are multiplied by the same number, 3, to get the second ratio.**

5. Explain one method you can use to determine if a relationship among quantities is proportional. **Sample answer: Find the unit rate of each relationship. If they are the same, then the relationship is proportional.**

Remember What You Learned

6. Work with a partner. Each of you should write about two different relationships, one which is proportional, and one that is not. Exchange what you wrote with your partner. Then determine which relationship is proportional and which one is not proportional. **See students' work.**

NAME _____ DATE _____ PERIOD _____

6-2 Enrichment

Business Planning

In order to have a successful business, the manager must plan ahead and decide how certain actions will affect the business. The first step is to predict the financial impact of business decisions. Julie has decided that she wants to start a brownie business to make extra money over the summer. Before she can ask her parents for money to start her business, she needs to have some information about how many batches of brownies she can make in a day and for how much she must sell the brownies to make a profit.

1. Julie can bake 3 batches of brownies in 2 hours. Her goal is to bake 12 batches of brownies each day. Use the table to find how many hours Julie will need to bake to reach her goal.

Batches of Brownies	3	6	9	12
Hours	2	4	6	8

2. Each batch of brownies will be sold for $2.00. How much money will Julie make if she sells 6 batches of brownies?

Batches of Brownies	1	2	3	4	5	6
Cost	$2	$4	$6	$8	$10	$12

3. If Julie works for 10 hours a day, how many batches of brownies can she bake?

Batches of Brownies	3	15
Hours	2	10

4. Julie hires a friend to help. Together, they can bake 24 batches of brownies in 8 hours. How long does it take for the two of them to bake 6 batches of brownies?

Batches of Brownies	6	12	18	24
Hours	2	4	6	8

5. If Julie and her friend can bake 24 batches of brownies in 8 hours, and they both work 40 hours in one week, how many batches of brownies can they bake that week? If Julie still charges $2.00 a batch, how much money will they make that week?

Hours	8	16	24	32	40
Batches of Brownies	24	48	72	96	120

Batches of Brownies	1	120
Cost	$2	$240

Answers

6-3 Skills Practice

Proportions

Determine if the quantities in each pair of ratios or rates are proportional. Explain your reasoning and express each proportional relationship as a proportion.

1. $18 for 3 bracelets; $30 for 5 bracelets

yes; $\dfrac{\$18}{3 \text{ bracelets}} = \dfrac{\$30}{5 \text{ bracelets}}$

2. 120 calories in 2 servings; 360 calories in 6 servings

yes; $\dfrac{120 \text{ calories}}{2 \text{ servings}} = \dfrac{360 \text{ calories}}{6 \text{ servings}}$

3. 4 hours worked for $12; 7 hours worked for $28   **no**

4. 15 blank CDs for $5; 45 blank CDs for $15   yes; $\dfrac{15 \text{ CDs}}{\$5} = \dfrac{45 \text{ CDs}}{\$15}$

5. 24 points scored in 4 games; 48 points scored in 10 games   **no**

6. 15 out of 20 students own hand-held games; 105 out of 160 students own hand-held games.   **no**

7. 30 minutes to jog 3 miles; 50 minutes to jog 5 miles   yes; $\dfrac{30 \text{ min}}{3 \text{ mi}} = \dfrac{50 \text{ min}}{5 \text{ mi}}$

8. $3 for 6 muffins; $9 for 18 muffins   yes; $\dfrac{\$3}{6 \text{ muffins}} = \dfrac{\$9}{18 \text{ muffins}}$

9. 360 miles driven on 12 gallons of fuel; 270 miles driven on 9 gallons of fuel   yes; $\dfrac{360 \text{ mi}}{12 \text{ gal}} = \dfrac{270 \text{ mi}}{9 \text{ gal}}$

10. 2 pairs of jeans for $50; 4 pairs of jeans for $90   **no**

6-3 Study Guide and Intervention

Proportions

Two quantities are said to be **proportional** if they have a constant ratio. A **proportion** is an equation stating that two ratios are equivalent.

Example 1 Determine if the quantities in each pair of rates are proportional. Explain your reasoning and express each proportional relationship as a proportion.

$35 for 7 balls of yarn; $24 for 4 balls of yarn.

Write each ratio as a fraction. Then find its unit rate.

$$\dfrac{\$35}{7 \text{ balls of yarn}} \overset{\div 7}{=} \dfrac{\$5}{1 \text{ ball of yarn}}$$

$$\dfrac{\$24}{4 \text{ balls of yarn}} \overset{\div 4}{=} \dfrac{\$6}{1 \text{ ball of yarn}}$$

Since the ratios do not share the same unit rate, the cost is not proportional to the number of balls of yarn purchased.

Example 2 Determine if the quantities in each pair of rates are proportional. Explain your reasoning and express each proportional relationship as a proportion.

8 boys out of 24 students; 4 boys out of 12 students

Write each ratio as a fraction.

$$\dfrac{8 \text{ boys}}{24 \text{ students}} \overset{\div 2}{=} \dfrac{4 \text{ boys}}{12 \text{ students}}$$ ← The numerator and the denominator are divided by the same number.

Since the fractions are equivalent, the number of boys is proportional to the number of students.

Exercises

Determine if the quantities in each pair of rates are proportional. Explain your reasoning and express each proportional relationship as a proportion.

1. $12 saved after 2 weeks; $36 saved after 6 weeks

yes; $\dfrac{\$12}{2 \text{ weeks}} = \dfrac{\$36}{6 \text{ weeks}}$

2. $9 for 3 magazines; $20 for 5 magazines   **no**

3. 135 miles driven in 3 hours; 225 miles driven in 5 hours

yes; $\dfrac{135 \text{ mi}}{3 \text{ h}} = \dfrac{225 \text{ mi}}{5 \text{ h}}$

4. 24 computers for 30 students; 48 computers for 70 students   **no**

6-3 Practice

Proportions

Determine if the quantities in each pair of ratios are proportional. Explain your reasoning and express each proportional relationship as a proportion.

1. 18 vocabulary words learned in 2 hours; 27 vocabulary words learned in 3 hours **Yes; since the ratios share the same unit rate, the number of words learned is proportional to the number of hours.** $\frac{18 \text{ words}}{2 \text{ hours}} = \frac{27 \text{ words}}{3 \text{ hours}}$

2. $15 for 5 pairs of socks; $25 for 10 pairs of socks **No; since the ratios do not share the same unit rate, the price is not proportional to the number of pairs of socks.**

3. 20 out of 45 students attended the concert; 12 out of 25 students attended the concert **No; since the fractions are not equivalent, the number of students who attended the concert is not proportional to the total number of students.**

4. 78 correct answers out of 100 test questions; 39 correct answers out of 50 test questions **Yes; since the fractions are equivalent, the number of correct answers is proportional to the number of questions on the test.** $\frac{78 \text{ correct answers}}{100 \text{ questions}} = \frac{39 \text{ correct answers}}{50 \text{ questions}}$

5. 15 minutes to drive 21 miles; 25 minutes to drive 35 miles **Yes; since the fractions are equivalent, the number of miles driven is proportional to the number of minutes.** $\frac{21 \text{ miles}}{15 \text{ minutes}} = \frac{35 \text{ miles}}{25 \text{ minutes}}$

ANIMALS For Exercises 6–8, refer to the table on lengths of some animals with long tails. Determine if each pair of animals has the same body length to tail length proportions. Explain your reasoning.

Animal Lengths (mm)		
Animal	**Head & Body**	**Tail**
Brown Rat	240	180
Hamster	250	50
Lemming	125	25
Opossum	480	360
Prairie Dog	280	40

6. brown rat and opossum **Yes; the ratios for the animals form equivalent fractions.**

7. hamster and lemming **Yes; the ratio for both animals have the same unit rate, $\frac{5 \text{ mm head \& body}}{1 \text{ mm tail}}$.**

8. opossum and prairie dog **No; the ratio for the opossum is $\frac{4}{3}$, but the ratio for the prairie dog is $\frac{7}{1}$. These are not equivalent fractions.**

6-3 Word Problem Practice

Proportions

1. **FITNESS** Jessica can do 60 jumping-jacks in 2 minutes. Juanita can do 150 jumping-jacks in 5 minutes. Are these rates proportional? Explain your reasoning. **Yes; The unit rate for each is $\frac{30 \text{ jumping jacks}}{1 \text{ min}}$.**

2. **BAKING** A cookie recipe that yields 48 cookies calls for 2 cups of flour. A different cookie recipe that yields 60 cookies calls for 3 cups of flour. Are these rates proportional? Explain your reasoning. **No; The unit rate for the first recipe is $\frac{24 \text{ cookies}}{1 \text{ cup flour}}$, and the unit rate for the second recipe is $\frac{20 \text{ cookies}}{1 \text{ cup flour}}$.**

3. **MUSIC** A music store is having a sale where you can buy 2 new-release CDs for $22 or you can buy 4 new-release CDs for $40. Are these rates proportional? Explain your reasoning. **No; the unit rate for buying 2 CDs is $\frac{\$11}{\text{CD}}$, and the unit rate for buying 4 CDs is $\frac{\$10}{\text{CD}}$.**

4. **TRAVEL** On the Mertler's vacation to Florida, they drove 180 miles in 3 hours before stopping for lunch. After lunch they drove 120 miles in 2 hours before stopping for gas. Are these rates proportional? Explain your reasoning. **Yes; The unit rate for each is $\frac{60 \text{ mi}}{1 \text{ h}}$.**

5. **BOOKS** At the school book sale, Michael bought 3 books for $6. Darnell bought 5 books for $10. Are these rates proportional? Explain your reasoning. **Yes; The fractions $\frac{3 \text{ books}}{\$6}$ and $\frac{5 \text{ books}}{\$10}$ are equivalent.**

6. **SURVEY** One school survey showed that 3 out of 5 students own a pet. Another survey showed that 6 out of 11 students own a pet. Are these results proportional? Explain your reasoning. **No; The fractions $\frac{3}{5}$ and $\frac{6}{11}$ are not equivalent.**

6-3 Enrichment

NAME _____ DATE _____ PERIOD _____

"Liberty Enlightening the World"

On July 4, 1889, in gratitude to the French for the gift of the Statue of Liberty, Americans from Paris gave to the French a miniature Statue of Liberty. The statue is made of bronze and is approximately one fourth the size of the original. This smaller-scale copy is found near the Grenelle Bridge on the Île des Cygnes, an island in the Seine River about one mile south of the Eiffel Tower.

1. If the original Statue of Liberty is approximately 150 feet tall, about how tall is the replica? **37.5 ft**

2. Complete the table. The first one is done for you.

	Original Statue of Liberty	Replica
Length of hand	16 ft	4 ft
Length of nose	4.5 ft	1.125 ft
Length of right arm	42 ft	10.5 ft
Head thickness from ear to ear	10 ft	2.5 ft
Width of mouth	3 ft	9 in.
Thickness of waist	35 ft	8.75 ft
Distance from heel to the top of her head	111 ft	27.75 ft
Length of index finger	8 ft	2 ft
Circumference of the second joint	3.5 ft	0.875 ft

3. The fingernail on the index finger of the original weighs 1.5 kilograms. How much does the fingernail on the replica in France weigh? **0.375 kg**

4. The dimensions of the tablet that Lady Liberty is holding are 23.6 feet by 13.6 feet by 2 feet. What are the dimensions of the smaller-scale tablet in France? **5.9 ft by 3.4 ft by 0.5 ft**

5. CHALLENGE The fingernail on the index finger is 13 inches long and 10 inches wide. What will be the area of the fingernail on the replica in France? **8.125 in²**

6-3 TI-73 Activity

NAME _____ DATE _____ PERIOD _____

Proportions

Cara and Jeff are going to cater a family reunion. Their recipe for potato salad serves 10 people. How much of each ingredient will they need to make enough for 75 people? You can use lists on your calculator to find the amount of each ingredient.

> **Mustard Potato Salad**
> $\frac{1}{2}$ c light mayonnaise
> 2 T Dijon mustard
> 2 T sweet pickle relish
> 1 T white vinegar
> $\frac{1}{4}$ t salt
> $\frac{1}{8}$ t pepper
> 5 c cooked potatoes
> $\frac{1}{4}$ c minced parsley
>
> Combine the first six ingredients in a large bowl. Add potatoes and toss. Cover and chill overnight. Garnish with parsley. Serves 10.

Example 1

Step 1 Clear all lists.
2nd [MEM] 6 ENTER
Open the list feature.
LIST

Step 2 Enter the recipe ingredient amounts in L1.
Use the $\frac{b}{c}$ key to enter fractions. Press ENTER after each value.

Step 3 Enter a formula in L2 to find the amount for 75 people. Use a proportion.

$$\frac{\text{Recipe Amount}}{10 \text{ people}} = \frac{x}{75 \text{ people}}$$

$$10x = (\text{Recipe Amount}) \times 75$$

$$x = (\text{Recipe Amount}) \times 75 \div 10 \quad \text{or} \quad x = L1 \times 75 \div 10$$

Use ▲ and ◄ to move to L2. Be sure you are on L2 and not L2(1).

Enter the formula.
2nd [TEXT] " Done ENTER ENTER 2nd [STAT] 1 × 75 ÷ 10 2nd [TEXT]
" Done ENTER ENTER

The amounts for 75 people are shown in L2. The amount of mayonnaise is $3\frac{3}{4}$ cups.

Exercises

Solve the following proportion questions.

1. Suppose you need to make enough potato salad for 45 people. Enter a new formula in L3 and find the amounts you need. Record the formula. List the amount of each ingredient.
L1 * $\frac{45}{10}$ or L1 * 45 ÷ 10; $2\frac{1}{4}$ c mayo, 9 T mustard, 9 T relish, $4\frac{1}{2}$ T vinegar, $1\frac{1}{8}$ t salt, $\frac{9}{16}$ t pepper, $22\frac{1}{2}$ c potatoes, $1\frac{1}{8}$ c parsley.

2. Suppose you decide that the original recipe would serve 12 people. You need to feed 30 people. Enter a new formula in L4 to find the amounts you need. Record the formula. List the amount of each ingredient.
L1 * $\frac{30}{12}$ or L1 * 30 ÷ 12; $1\frac{1}{4}$ c mayo, 5 T mustard, 5 T relish, $2\frac{1}{2}$ T vinegar, $\frac{5}{8}$ t salt, $\frac{5}{16}$ t pepper, $12\frac{1}{2}$ c potatoes, $\frac{5}{8}$ c parsley.

NAME _____ DATE _____ PERIOD _____

6-4 Study Guide and Intervention
Algebra: Solving Proportions

To *solve a proportion* means to find the unknown value in the proportion. By examining how the numerators or denominators of the proportion are related, you can perform an operation on one fraction to create an equivalent fraction.

Example 1 Solve $\frac{3}{4} = \frac{b}{12}$.

Find a value for b that would make the fractions equivalent.

$$\frac{3}{4} \underset{\times 3}{\overset{\times 3}{=}} \frac{b}{12} \qquad \text{Since } 4 \times 3 = 12, \text{ multiply the numerator and denominator by 3.}$$

$b = 3 \times 3$ or 9

Example 2 NUTRITION Three servings of broccoli contain 150 calories. How many servings of broccoli contain 250 calories?

Set up the proportion. Let a represent the number of servings that contain 250 calories.

$$\frac{150 \text{ calories}}{3 \text{ servings}} = \frac{250 \text{ calories}}{a \text{ servings}}$$

Find the unit rate.

$$\frac{150 \text{ calories}}{3 \text{ servings}} \underset{\div 3}{\overset{\div 3}{=}} \frac{50 \text{ calories}}{1 \text{ serving}}$$

Rewrite the proportion using the unit rate and solve using equivalent fractions.

$$\frac{50 \text{ calories}}{1 \text{ serving}} \underset{\times 5}{\overset{\times 5}{=}} \frac{250 \text{ calories}}{5 \text{ servings}}$$

So, 5 servings of broccoli contain 250 calories.

Exercises

Solve each proportion.

1. $\frac{2}{3} = \frac{8}{n}$ **12**
2. $\frac{2}{4} = \frac{y}{8}$ **4**
3. $\frac{3}{5} = \frac{b}{15}$ **9**
4. $\frac{4}{5} = \frac{16}{w}$ **20**
5. $\frac{d}{16} = \frac{3}{8}$ **6**
6. $\frac{2}{y} = \frac{6}{9}$ **3**

7. MUSIC Jeremy spent $33 on 3 CDs. At this rate, how much would 5 CDs cost?   **$55**

NAME _____ DATE _____ PERIOD _____

6-4 Lesson Reading Guide
Algebra: Solving Proportions

Get Ready for the Lesson

Read the introduction at the top of page 334 in your textbook. Write your answers below.

1. How many pairs of flip flops can you buy with $20? $25?
4; 5

2. Write a proportion to express the relationship between the cost of 3 pairs of flip flops and the cost c of 7 pairs of flip flops.
$\frac{3}{\$15} = \frac{7}{\$c}$

3. How much will it cost to buy 6 pairs of flip flops?
$30

Read the Lesson

4. In Example 1, explain why you multiply by 5 to solve the proportion. **Sample answer: You know that the denominator of a fraction equivalent to $\frac{4}{7}$ is 35, and by multiplying the numerator and denominator by the same value, 5, you can obtain the new numerator.**

5. Look at the final sentence in Example 4 on page 335— "So, about 400 out of 500 people can be expected to prefer eating at a restaurant." Why is it important to use *can be expected* in this answer? **Sample answer: Because this is a prediction; there is no way of knowing for sure the preference of all 500 people unless each one is questioned individually.**

Remember What You Learned

6. Work with a partner. Study Examples 1–3 on pages 334 and 335. Write a proportion that needs to be solved for an unknown value. Exchange proportions and solve for the unknown value. Explain how you arrived at your solution. **See students' work.**

Answers

Skills Practice

NAME _____ DATE _____ PERIOD _____

6-4 Skills Practice

Algebra: Solving Proportions

Solve each proportion.

1. $\frac{2}{5} = \frac{8}{x}$ **20**
2. $\frac{2}{7} = \frac{4}{y}$ **14**
3. $\frac{3}{5} = \frac{b}{30}$ **18**
4. $\frac{2}{9} = \frac{c}{36}$ **8**
5. $\frac{4}{5} = \frac{d}{25}$ **20**
6. $\frac{20}{4} = \frac{10}{f}$ **2**
7. $\frac{g}{2} = \frac{28}{14}$ **4**
8. $\frac{2}{x} = \frac{10}{25}$ **5**
9. $\frac{4}{3} = \frac{h}{18}$ **24**
10. $\frac{10}{30} = \frac{2}{r}$ **6**
11. $\frac{t}{18} = \frac{3}{6}$ **9**
12. $\frac{2}{3} = \frac{6}{m}$ **9**
13. $\frac{9}{2} = \frac{s}{6}$ **27**
14. $\frac{n}{36} = \frac{2}{6}$ **12**
15. $\frac{4}{u} = \frac{12}{21}$ **7**
16. $\frac{5}{6} = \frac{m}{12}$ **10**
17. $\frac{d}{27} = \frac{4}{9}$ **12**
18. $\frac{5}{8} = \frac{15}{q}$ **24**
19. $\frac{15}{27} = \frac{5}{k}$ **9**
20. $\frac{4}{x} = \frac{20}{30}$ **6**
21. $\frac{b}{3} = \frac{24}{9}$ **8**
22. $\frac{z}{35} = \frac{4}{7}$ **20**
23. $\frac{6}{c} = \frac{24}{28}$ **7**
24. $\frac{6}{8} = \frac{x}{24}$ **18**
25. $\frac{14}{16} = \frac{b}{8}$ **7**
26. $\frac{8}{r} = \frac{24}{27}$ **9**
27. $\frac{16}{36} = \frac{t}{9}$ **4**

Practice

NAME _____ DATE _____ PERIOD _____

6-4 Practice

Algebra: Solving Proportions

Solve each proportion.

1. $\frac{2}{3} = \frac{n}{21}$ **14**
2. $\frac{2}{x} = \frac{16}{40}$ **5**
3. $\frac{80}{100} = \frac{b}{5}$ **4**
4. $\frac{m}{2} = \frac{75}{50}$ **3**
5. $\frac{6}{5} = \frac{42}{a}$ **35**
6. $\frac{3}{d} = \frac{21}{56}$ **8**
7. $\frac{4}{3} = \frac{f}{45}$ **60**
8. $\frac{h}{12} = \frac{70}{120}$ **7**
9. $\frac{3}{5} = \frac{27}{p}$ **45**
10. $\frac{26}{21} = \frac{r}{63}$ **78**
11. $\frac{17}{y} = \frac{102}{222}$ **37**
12. $\frac{7}{10} = \frac{c}{25}$ **17.5**

13. **MAMMALS** A pronghorn antelope can travel 105 miles in 3 hours. If it continued traveling at the same speed, how far could a pronghorn travel in 11 hours? **385 mi**

14. **BIKES** Out of 32 students in a class, 5 said they ride their bikes to school. Based on these results, predict how many of the 800 students in the school ride their bikes to school. **125 students**

15. **MEAT** Hamburger sells for 3 pounds for $6. If Alicia buys 10 pounds of hamburger, how much will she pay? **$20**

16. **FOOD** If 24 extra large cans of soup will serve 96 people, how many cans should Ann buy to serve 28 people? **7 cans**

17. **BIRDS** The ruby throated hummingbird has a wing beat of about 200 beats per second. About how many wing beats would a hummingbird have in 3 minutes? **about 36,000 wing beats**

NAME _____ DATE _____ PERIOD _____

6-4 Word Problem Practice
Algebra: Solving Proportions

1. SCHOOL The ratio of boys to girls in history class is 4 to 5. How many girls are in the class if there are 12 boys in the class? Explain.
15 girls; Sample answer: If the ratio is 4 boys for every 5 girls in the class, the equivalent ratio must be 12 boys to an unknown number of girls, $\frac{4}{5} = \frac{12}{g}$. Since $12 = 3 \times 4$, $g = 3 \times 5$ or 15.

2. FACTORIES A factory produces 6 motorcycles in 9 hours. Write a proportion and solve it to find how many hours it takes to produce 16 motorcycles.
$\frac{6}{9} = \frac{16}{x}$; **24 h**

3. READING James read 4 pages in a book in 6 minutes. How long would you expect him to take to read 6 pages?
9 min

4. COOKING A recipe that will make 3 pies calls for 7 cups of flour. Write a proportion and solve it to find how many pies can be made with 28 cups of flour.
$\frac{3}{7} = \frac{p}{28}$; **12 pies**

5. TYPING Sara can type 90 words in 4 minutes. About how many words would you expect her to type in 10 minutes? **225 words**

6. BASKETBALL The Lakewood Wildcats won 5 of their first 7 games this year. There are 28 games in the season. About how many games would you expect the Wildcats to win this season? Explain your reasoning.
20 games; Sample answer: If they have already won 5 out of 7 games, they will probably continue to win in the same proportion for the remainder of the season, $\frac{5}{7} = \frac{x}{28}$.

7. FOOD Two slices of Dan's Famous Pizza have 230 Calories. How many Calories would you expect to be in 5 slices of the same pizza?
575 Calories

8. SHOPPING Andy paid $12 for 4 baseball card packs. Write a proportion and solve it to find how many baseball card packs he can purchase for $21.
$\frac{\$12}{4} = \frac{\$21}{x}$; **7 packs**

Lesson 6-4

NAME _____ DATE _____ PERIOD _____

6-4 Enrichment

Ada

Did you know that a woman wrote the first description of a computer programming language? She was the daughter of a famous English lord and was born in 1815. She had a deep understanding of mathematics and was fascinated by calculating machines. Her interests led her to create the first algorithm. In 1843, she translated a French version of a lecture by Charles Babbage. In her notes to the translation, she outlined the fundamental concepts of computer programming. She died in 1852. In 1979, the U.S. Department of Defense named the computer language *Ada* after her.

To find out this woman's full name, solve the proportion for each letter.

1. $\frac{7}{A} = \frac{28}{40}$ **10** **2.** $\frac{5}{4} = \frac{B}{36}$ **45** **3.** $\frac{1}{3} = \frac{C}{15}$ **5**

4. $\frac{5}{D} = \frac{35}{63}$ **9** **5.** $\frac{2}{5} = \frac{E}{20}$ **8** **6.** $\frac{2}{18} = \frac{L}{27}$ **3**

7. $\frac{6}{N} = \frac{12}{14}$ **7** **8.** $\frac{9}{11} = \frac{O}{44}$ **36** **9.** $\frac{2}{8} = \frac{R}{4}$ **1**

10. $\frac{5}{V} = \frac{25}{30}$ **6** **11.** $\frac{7}{4} = \frac{Y}{28}$ **49**

Now look for each solution below. Write the corresponding letter on the line above the solution. If you have calculated correctly, the letters will spell her name.

A	D	A		B	Y	R	O	N
$\frac{A}{10}$	$\frac{D}{9}$	$\frac{A}{10}$		$\frac{B}{45}$	$\frac{Y}{49}$	$\frac{R}{1}$	$\frac{O}{36}$	$\frac{N}{7}$

L	O	V	E	L	A	C	E
$\frac{L}{3}$	$\frac{O}{36}$	$\frac{V}{6}$	$\frac{E}{8}$	$\frac{L}{3}$	$\frac{A}{10}$	$\frac{C}{5}$	$\frac{E}{8}$

Answers

Answers (Lesson 6-5)

6-5 Skills Practice

Problem-Solving Investigation: Look for a Pattern

Solve. Use the look for a pattern strategy.

1. **NUMBER SENSE** Describe the pattern below, Then find the missing number.

1, 20, 400, __?__, 160,000

Each number is 20 times the previous number. The missing number is 8,000.

2. **GEOMETRY** Use the pattern below to find the perimeter of the eighth figure. **20**

Figure 1   Figure 2   Figure 3

3. **PHYSICAL SCIENCE** A cup of marbles hangs from a rubber band. The length of the rubber band is measured as shown in the graph at the right. Predict the approximate length of the rubber band if 6 marbles are in the cup.
about 15 cm

Rubber Band Stretch

Length (cm)

15
10
5
0

0 1 2 3 4
Number of Marbles

4. **ALLOWANCE** In 2002, Estella earned $200 in allowance, and Kelsey earned $150 in allowance. Each year Kelsey earned $20 more in allowance, and Estella earned $10 more. In what year will they earn the same amount of money? How much will it be? **2007; $250**

Chapter 6   35   Course 1

6-5 Study Guide and Intervention

Problem-Solving Investigation: Look for a Pattern

When solving problems, one strategy that is helpful is to *look for a pattern*. In some problem situations, you can extend and examine a pattern in order to solve the problem.

You can use the *look for a pattern* strategy, along with the following four-step problem solving plan to solve a problem.

1 **Understand** – Read and get a general understanding of the problem.
2 **Plan** – Make a plan to solve the problem and estimate the solution.
3 **Solve** – Use your plan to solve the problem.
4 **Check** – Check the reasonableness of your solution.

Example MEDICINE Monisha has the flu. The doctor gave her medicine to take over the next 2 weeks. The first 3 days she is to take 2 pills a day. Then the remaining days she is to take 1 pill. How many pills will Monisha have taken at the end of the 2 weeks?

Understand You know she is to take the medicine for 2 weeks. You also know she is to take 2 pills the first 3 days and then only 1 pill the remaining days. You need to find the total number of pills.

Plan Start with the first week and look for a pattern.

Solve

Day	1	2	3	4	5	6	7
Number of Pills	2	2	2	1	1	1	1
Total Pills	2	$2 + 2 = 4$	$4 + 2 = 6$	$6 + 1 = 7$	$7 + 1 = 8$	$8 + 1 = 9$	$9 + 1 = 10$

After the first few days the number of pills increases by 1. You can add 7 more pills to the total for the first week, $10 + 7 = 17$. So, by the end of the 2 weeks, Monisha will have taken 17 pills to get over the flu.

Check You can extend the table for the next 7 days to check the answer.

Exercise

TIME Buses arrive every 30 minutes at the bus stop. The first bus arrives at 6:20 A.M. Hogan wants to get on the first bus after 8:00 A.M. What time will the bus that Hogan wants to take arrive at the bus stop? **8:20 A.M.**

Chapter 6   34   Course 1

6-5 Practice

Problem-Solving Investigation: Look for a Pattern

Mixed Problem Solving

Use the look for a pattern strategy to solve Exercises 1 and 2.

1. MONEY In 2005, Trey had $7,200 in his saving-for-college account and Juan had $8,000. Each year, Trey will add $400 and Juan will add $200. In what year will they both have the same amount of money in their accounts, not counting interest earned? How much will it be? **2009; $8,800**

2. BUTTONS Draw the next two figures in the pattern below.

4. NUMBER SENSE Describe the pattern below. Then find the missing number.

5,000, 2,500, ■, 625,. . . .

Each number is half the previous number; 1,250

5. TRAVEL An express bus left the station at 6:30 a.m. and arrived at its destination at 12:00 noon. It traveled a distance of 260 miles and made only one stop for a half hour to drop off and pick up passengers. What was the average speed of the bus? **52 mph**

6. MONEY Len bought a $24.99 pair of pants and paid a total of $27.05, including tax. How much was the tax? **$2.06**

7. PHOTOGRAPHY Ms. Julian gives photography workshops. She collected $540 in fees for a workshop attended by 12 participants. Ms. Julian spent $15 per person for supplies for them and herself and $6 per person for box lunches for them and herself. How much money did Ms. Julian have left as profit? **$267**

Use any strategy to solve Exercises 3–7. Some strategies are shown below.

Problem-Solving Strategies
• Guess and check.
• Look for a pattern.
• Act it out.

3. MUSIC Last week Jason practiced playing his bassoon for 95 minutes. This week he practiced 5 more minutes than 3 times the number of minutes he practiced last week. How many minutes did Jason practice this week? **290 min**

6-5 Word Problem Practice

Problem-Solving Investigation: Look for a Pattern

1. HEIGHT Fernando is 2 inches taller than Jason. Jason is 1.5 inches shorter than Kendra and 1 inch taller than Nicole. Hao, who is 5 feet 10 inches tall, is 2.5 inches taller than Fernando. How tall is each student?
Hao is 5'10"; Fernando is 5'7.5"; Kendra is 5'7"; Jason is 5'5.5"; and Nicole is 5'4.5".

2. FRUIT The table below shows the results of a survey of students' favorite fruit. How many more students like apples than bananas? **1**

Favorite Fruit				
A	B	G	B	A
O	A	G	G	A
G	O	A	B	O

A = apple   B = banana   G = grapes
O = orange

3. MONEY Dominic's mother gave him $20 to go to the grocery store. If the groceries cost $12.56, how much change will he receive? **$7.44**

4. BOOKS An author has written 4 different books. Each book is available in hard bound, soft bound, and on tape. How many different items are available by this author? **12**

5. FOOTBALL The varsity football team scored 24 points in last Friday's game. They scored a combination of 7-point touchdowns and 3-point field goals. How many touchdowns and how many field goals did they score? **3 touchdowns and 1 field goal**

6. CYCLING Jody and Lazaro are cycling in a 24-mile race. Jody is cycling at an average speed of 8 miles per hour. Lazaro is cycling at an average speed of 6 miles per hour. If they both started the race at the same time, who will finish first? How much faster will they finish the race?
Jody will finish the race first. She will finish 1 hour before Lazaro.

Answers

NAME _____ DATE _____ PERIOD _____

6-6 Study Guide and Intervention

Sequences and Expressions

A **sequence** is a list of numbers in a specific order. Each number in the sequence is called a **term**. An **arithmetic sequence** is a sequence in which each term is found by adding the same number to the previous term.

Example Use words and symbols to describe the value of each term as a function of its position. Then find the value of the tenth term in the sequence.

Position	1	2	3	4	n
Value of Term	4	8	12	16	?

Study the relationship between each position and the value of its term.

Notice that the value of each term is 4 times its position number. So the value of the term in position n is $4n$.

Position		Value of term
1	$\times 4 =$	4
2	$\times 4 =$	8
3	$\times 4 =$	12
4	$\times 4 =$	16
n	$\times 4 =$	$4n$

To find the value of the tenth term, replace n with 10 in the algebraic expression $4n$. Since $4 \times 10 = 40$, the value of the tenth term in the sequence is 40.

Exercises

Use words and symbols to describe the value of each term as a function of its position. Then find the value of the tenth term in the sequence.

1.

Position	3	4	5	6	n
Value of Term	1	2	3	4	?

subtract 2; $n - 2$; 8

2.

Position	1	2	3	4	n
Value of Term	5	10	15	20	?

multiply by 5; $5n$; 50

3.

Position	4	5	6	7	n
Value of Term	11	12	13	14	?

add 7; $n + 7$; 17

NAME _____ DATE _____ PERIOD _____

6-6 Lesson Reading Guide

Sequences and Expressions

Get Ready for the Lesson

Read the introduction at the top of page 243 in your textbook. Write your answers below.

1. Find the rate of slices to the number of pizzas for each row in the table.
$\frac{8}{1}, \frac{16}{2}, \frac{24}{3}, \frac{32}{4}$

2. Is the number of pizzas proportional to the number of slices? Explain your reasoning. **The ratio of slices to number of pizzas for all rows are equal to 8; therefore, the number of pizzas is proportional to the number of slices.**

3. Make an ordered list of the number of slices and describe the pattern between consecutive numbers in this list. **8, 16, 24, 32; Each number in the list is 8 more than the previous number.**

4. What relationship appears to exist between the pattern found in Exercise 3 and the rates found in Exercise 1? **The number added to find the next term in the list appears to be equal to the ratio** number of slices / number of pizzas.

Read the Lesson

5. If you have a list of numbers, how can you tell if they are an arithmetic sequence? **They will be a list of numbers in a specific order in which each term is found by adding the same number to the previous term.**

6. In extending a sequence, how can you use an algebraic expression to find the tenth term? **First find the relationship that exists between each position and the value of the term. Next use n to write an algebraic expression for this relationship. Then replace n with 10 to find the tenth term.**

Remember What You Learned

7. Work with a partner. Make up a sequence of numbers that follow a certain pattern. Exchange lists with your partner. For the list you receive from your partner, describe the pattern, write a function describing the pattern, and then find the tenth term in the pattern. **See students' work.**

Answers (Lesson 6-6)

6-6 Practice

Sequences and Expressions

Use words and symbols to describe the value of each term as a function of its position. Then find the value of the sixteenth term in the sequence.

1.

Position	2	3	4	5	n	■
Value of Term	8	12	16	20		■

Multiply by 4; $4n$; 64

2.

Position	8	9	10	11	n	■
Value of Term	14	15	16	17		■

Add 6; $n + 6$; 22

3.

Position	11	12	13	14	n	■
Value of Term	4	5	6	7		■

Subtract 7; $n - 7$; 9

4.

Position	21	22	23	24	n	■
Value of Term	12	13	14	15		■

Subtract 9; $n - 9$; 7

Determine how the next term in each sequence can be found. Then find the next two terms in the sequence.

5. 3, 16, 29, 42, ... **Add 13; 55, 68**

6. 29, 25, 21, 17, ... **Subtract 4; 13, 9**

7. 1, 2, 3.5, 5.8, 8.1, ... **Add 2.3; 10.4, 12.7**

Find the missing number in each sequence.

8. 5, 10, $12\frac{1}{2}$, ... $7\frac{1}{2}$

9. 11.5, 9.4, ■, 5.2 **7.3**

10. 40, ■, $37\frac{1}{3}$, 36, ... $38\frac{2}{3}$

11. MEASUREMENT There are 52 weeks in 1 year. In the space at the right, make a table and write an algebraic expression relating the number of weeks to the number of years. Then find Hana's age in weeks if she is 11 years old. **572 weeks**

Weeks	Years
52	1
104	2
156	3
52n	n

12. COMPUTERS There are about 8 bits of digital information in 1 byte. In the space at the right, make a table and write an algebraic expression relating the number of bits to the number of bytes. Then find the number of bits there are in one kilobyte if there are 1,024 bytes in one kilobyte. **8,192 bits**

Bits	Bytes
8	1
16	2
24	3
8n	n

6-6 Skills Practice

Sequences and Expressions

Use words and symbols to describe the value of each term as a function of its position. Then find the value of the tenth term in the sequence.

1.

Position	5	6	7	8	n
Value of Term	2	3	4	5	?

subtract 3; $n - 3$; 7

2.

Position	1	2	3	4	n
Value of Term	6	12	18	24	?

multiply by 6; $6n$; 60

3.

Position	1	2	3	4	n
Value of Term	10	11	12	13	?

add 9; $n + 9$; 19

4.

Position	1	2	3	4	n
Value of Term	4	8	12	16	?

multiply by 4; $4n$; 40

5.

Position	5	6	7	8	n
Value of Term	0	1	2	3	?

subtract 5; $n - 5$; 5

6.

Position	2	4	6	8	n
Value of Term	14	16	18	20	?

add 12; $n + 12$; 22

7.

Position	5	6	7	8	n
Value of Term	1	2	3	4	?

subtract 4; $n - 4$; 6

8.

Position	1	2	3	4	n
Value of Term	11	22	33	44	?

multiply by 11; $11n$; 110

Answers (Lesson 6-6)

6-6 Enrichment

Geometric Sequences

A geometric sequence is one in which the ratio between the two terms is constant.

1. SQUARE NUMBERS A square number can be modeled by using an area model to create an actual square.

a. Draw the next two terms in the sequence and determine the fourth term.

1   4   9   ? **16**

b. The function that describes square numbers is n^2. Write this function using multiplication. **$n \times n$**

c. Complete the table by finding the missing position and the missing value of the term for square numbers.

Position	3	8	**10**	11	**13**	15	25
Value of Term	9	64	100	**121**	**169**	225	625

2. TRIANGULAR NUMBERS A triangular number can be modeled by using manipulatives or objects to create triangles. The first three triangular numbers are 1, 3, and 6.

1   3   6   10   15   21

a. Draw the next three terms in the sequence in the space above.

b. What is the ninth term? **45**

c. The function that describes the triangular number sequence is $n \times \frac{(n+1)}{2}$. Complete the table by finding either the missing position or missing value of the term for triangular numbers.

Position	3	**4**	8	10	15	**20**	100
Value of Term	6	10	**36**	55	120	210	**5,050**

6-6 Word Problem Practice

Sequences and Expressions

1. AGE There are 12 months in 1 year. If Juan is 11 years old, how many months old is he? Make a table then write an algebraic expression relating the number of months to the number of years. **132 months**

Months	Year
12	1
24	2
36	3
12*n*	*n*

2. MEASUREMENT There are 12 inches in 1 foot. The height of Rachel's door is 7 feet. Find the height in inches. Make a table then write an algebraic expression relating the number of feet to inches. **84 in.**

Inches	Feet
12	1
24	2
36	3
12*n*	*n*

3. RUNNING There are 60 seconds in 1 minute. Pete can run all the way around the track in 180 seconds. Find how long it takes Pete to run around the track in minutes. Make a table then write an algebraic expression relating the number of seconds to the number of minutes. **3 minutes**

Seconds	Minutes
60	1
120	2
180	3
n	*n* ÷ 60

4. FRUIT There are 16 ounces in 1 pound. Chanda picked 9 pounds of cherries from her tree this year. Find the number of ounces of cherries Chanda picked. Make a table then write an algebraic expression relating the number of ounces to the number of pounds. **144 oz**

Ounces	Pounds
16	1
32	2
48	3
16*n*	*n*

5. SPORTS There are 3 feet in 1 yard. Tanya Streeter holds the world record for free-diving in the ocean. She dove 525 feet in $3\frac{1}{2}$ minutes. Find the number of yards she dove. Make a table then write an algebraic expression relating the number of feet to the number of yards. **175 yd**

Feet	Yards
3	1
6	2
9	3
n	*n* ÷ 3

6. COOKING There are 8 fluid ounces in 1 cup. A beef stew recipe calls for 3 cups of vegetable juice. Find the number of fluid ounces of vegetable juice needed for the recipe. Make a table then write an algebraic expression relating the number of fluid ounces to the number of cups. **24 fl oz**

Fluid Ounces	Cups
8	1
16	2
24	3
8*n*	*n*

Lesson 6-7

NAME _____ DATE _____ PERIOD _____

6-7 Lesson Reading Guide

Proportions and Equations

Get Ready for the Lesson

Read the introduction at the top of page 349 in your textbook. Write your answers below.

1. Write a sentence that describes the relationship between the number of hours she babysits and her earnings.
Carli earns $5 for every hour of babysitting.

2. Is the relationship proportional? Explain.
Yes; each quantity has a constant ratio of $\frac{1\,h}{\$5}$.

3. What is the rule to find the amount Carli earns for babysitting h hours? **5h**

4. If e represents the amount Carli earns, what equation can you use to represent this situation? **e = 5h**

Read the Lesson

5. What is the difference between an input value and an output value of a function?
The input value is the number that one or more operations is performed on, and the output is the resulting value.

6. Explain the steps involved in using an equation to represent a function. **First examine how the value of each input and output changes. Then write an algebraic expression for this relationship. Finally, set the algebraic expression equal to a variable, say y.**

Remember What You Learned

7. Work with a partner. Create a function table that can be represented with an equation. Exchange function tables with your partner. For the table you receive from your partner, write an equation to represent the function. **See students' work.**

Chapter 6   45   *Course 1*

NAME _____ DATE _____ PERIOD _____

6-6 Spreadsheet Activity

Sequences

You can use a spreadsheet to find the pattern in a sequence of numbers and to find the next two numbers in the sequence.

Example Use a spreadsheet to describe the pattern and find the next two terms in the sequence 22, 19, 16, 13, ...

Use the first row of the spreadsheet to enter the data. Enter the numbers using the formula bar. Click on a cell of the spreadsheet, type the number and press TAB.

Find the pattern of the sequence in the cell after the last number of the sequence. Since each term is decreased by the same amount, enter an equals sign followed by D1−C1. Then press ENTER. This returns a value of −3. Each term is 3 less than the term before it.

Find the next two terms in the sequence in the two cells next to the −3. Enter the formula =D1+E1. Then press ENTER. This returns the value of 10. Repeat this process to find the next term. Enter =F1+E1. This returns a value of 7. So, the next two terms in the sequence are 10 and 7.

◇	A	B	C	D	E	F	G	H
1	22	19	16	13	−3	10	7	
2								
3								

Sheet 1 / Sheet 2 / Sheet 3

Exercises

Use a spreadsheet to describe the pattern in each sequence. Then find the next two terms.

1. −6, −4, −2, 0, . . .
Add 2; 2, 4.

2. 2.5, 5, 7.5, 10, . . .
Add 2.5; 12.5, 15.

3. $\frac{1}{2}$, $\frac{1}{4}$, 0, $-\frac{1}{4}$, . . .
Subtract $\frac{1}{4}$; $-\frac{1}{2}$, $-\frac{3}{4}$

4. 12, 14, 16, 18, . . .
Add 2; 20, 22.

5. 5.5, 2.5, −0.5, −3.5, . . .
Subtract 3; −6.5, −9.5.

6. 1.2, 6.2, 11.2, 16.2, . . .
Add 5; 21.2, 26.2.

7. 2.1, 4.3, 6.5, 8.7, . . .
Add 2.2; 10.9, 13.1.

8. −4.4, −6.1, −7.8, −9.5, . . .
Subtract 1.7; −11.2, −12.9.

Chapter 6   44   *Course 1*

Answers

Answers (Lesson 6-7)

6-7 Skills Practice

NAME _____ DATE _____ PERIOD _____

Proportions and Equations

Write an equation to represent the function displayed in each table.

1.

Input, x	0	1	2	3	4
Output, y	0	3	6	9	12

$y = 3x$

2.

Input, x	0	1	2	3	4
Output, y	0	1	2	3	4

$y = x$

3.

Input, x	1	2	3	4	5
Output, y	7	14	21	28	35

$y = 7x$

4.

Input, x	0	1	2	3	4
Output, y	0	10	20	30	40

$y = 10x$

5.

Input, x	2	4	6	8	10
Output, y	4	8	12	16	20

$y = 2x$

6.

Input, x	0	1	2	3	4
Output, y	0	12	24	36	48

$y = 12x$

7.

Input, x	0	1	2	3	4
Output, y	0	8	16	24	32

$y = 8x$

8.

Input, x	0	1	2	3	4
Output, y	0	20	40	60	80

$y = 20x$

ANIMALS Use the following information for Exercises 9–11.

A manatee eats an average of 70 pounds of wet vegetation each day.

9. Make a table to show the relationship between the number of p pounds of wet vegetation a manatee eats in d days.

Number of Days, d	Total Pounds, p
1	70
2	140
3	210
4	280

10. Write an equation to find p, the number of pounds of wet vegetation a manatee eats in d days. $p = 70d$

11. How many pounds of wet vegetation does a manatee eat in 7 days? **490 lb**

Chapter 6　　47　　*Course 1*

6-7 Study Guide and Intervention

NAME _____ DATE _____ PERIOD _____

Proportions and Equations

A *function table* displays *input* and *output* values that represent a function. The function displayed in a function table can be represented with an *equation*.

Example 1 **Write an equation to represent the function displayed in the table.**

Input, x	1	2	3	4	5
Output, y	5	10	15	20	25

Examine how the value of each input and output changes.

Input, x	1	2	3	4	5
Output, y	5	10	15	20	25

As each input increases by 1, the output increases by 5. That is, the constant rate of change is 5.

So, the equation that represents the function is $y = 5x$.

Example 2 **Theo earns $6 an hour mowing lawns for his neighbors. Make a table and write an equation for the total amount t Theo earns for mowing h hours. How much will Theo earn for mowing lawns for 11 hours?**

As the number of hours increases by 1, the total earned increases by 6.

Hours, h	Total earned, t
1	$6
2	$12
3	$18
4	$24

So, the equation is $t = 6h$.

Let $h = 11$ to find how much Theo will earn in 11 hours.

$t = 6h$
$t = 6 \times 11$ or $66

Exercises

Write an equation to represent the function displayed in each table.

1.

Input, x	1	2	3	4	5
Output, y	2	4	6	8	10

$y = 2x$

2.

Input, x	0	1	2	3	4
Output, y	0	6	12	18	24

$y = 6x$

MUSIC Use the following information for Exercises 3–5.

A music store sells each used CD for $4.

3. Make a table to show the relationship between the number of c used CDs purchased and the total cost t. **See students' work.**

4. Write an equation to find t, the total cost in dollars for buying c used CDs. $t = 4c$

5. How much will it cost to buy 5 used CDs? **$20**

Chapter 6　　46　　*Course 1*

6-7 Word Problem Practice
Proportions and Equations

FITNESS For Exercises 1–3, use the following information.
Rosalia burns 250 Calories for each hour she does aerobics.

1. Make a table to show the relationship between the number of Calories c Rosalia burns doing aerobics for h hours.

Number of Hours, h	Calories Burned, c
1	250
2	500
3	750
4	1,000

2. Write an equation to find c, the number of Calories Rosalia burns in h hours.
$c = 250h$

3. If Rosalia goes to a 1-hour aerobic class 3 times a week, how many Calories will she burn each week doing aerobics?
750 Calories

4. MUSICALS The table below shows the admission price to the school musical. Write a sentence and an equation to describe the data. **The admission price for one person is $6; t = $6n.**

Number of People, n	Total Admission, t
1	$6
2	$12
3	$18

5. MUSICALS In Exercise 4, how much will it cost for a family of 5 to attend the musical? **$30**

6. VIDEO GAMES The table below shows the number of points earned for catching bugs in a video game. Write a sentence and an equation to describe the data. **You earn 25 points for each bug you catch; t = 25b**

Number of Bugs Caught, b	Total Points, t
1	25
2	50
3	75

6-7 Practice
Proportions and Equations

Write an equation to represent the function displayed in each table.

1.

Input, x	1	2	3	4	5
Output, y	7	14	21	28	35

$y = 7x$

2.

Input, x	0	1	2	3	4
Output, y	0	9	18	27	36

$y = 9x$

3.

Input, x	1	2	3	4	5
Output, y	13	26	39	52	65

$y = 13x$

4.

Input, x	10	20	30	40	50
Output, y	1	2	3	4	5

$y = x \div 10$

5.

Input, x	0	1	2	3	4
Output, y	0	14	28	42	56

$y = 14x$

6.

Input, x	4	8	12	16	20
Output, y	1	2	3	4	5

$y = x \div 4$

7.

Input, x	12	24	36	48	60
Output, y	1	2	3	4	5

$y = x \div 12$

8.

Input, x	6	12	18	24	30
Output, y	1	2	3	4	5

$y = x \div 6$

BATS Use the following information for Exercises 9–11.
A Little Brown Myotis bat can eat 500 mosquitoes in an hour.

9. In the space at the right, make a table to show the the relationship between the number of hours h and the number of mosquitoes eaten m.

Number of Hours, h	Number of Mosquitoes Eaten, m
1	500
2	1,000
3	1,500
4	2,000

10. Write an equation to find m, the number of mosquitoes a bat eats in h hours. **m = 500h**

11. How many mosquitoes can a Little Brown Myotis bat eat in 7 hours?
3,500 mosquitoes

12. RECREATION A community center charges the amount shown in the table for using specialized exercise equipment. Write a sentence and an equation to describe the data. How much will it cost to use the exercise equipment for 6 months? **It costs $20 per month to use the specialized exercise equipment; c = $20m; $120**

Number of Months, m	Cost, c
1	$20
2	$40
3	$60

Answers

Answers (Lesson 6-7)

NAME _____ DATE _____ PERIOD _____

6-7 Enrichment

Enchanted Rock

Enchanted Rock is a pink granite dome located in Enchanted Rock State Natural Area in Central Texas. It is of the largest batholiths in the United States. A batholith is made of igneous rock and is the result of volcanic activity. The Enchanted Rock dome rises 425 feet above the ground and is 1825 feet above sea level.

The entrance fee to Enchanted Rock State Natural Area is $5.00 per person.

1. Complete the table to find the entrance cost for groups of different sizes.

Input, x	1	2	3	4	5	6	7	8
Output, y	$5.00	$10.00	$15.00	$20.00	$25.00	$30.00	$35.00	$40.00

2. Write an equation to represent the function displayed in the table.
y = 5x

3. If the park has 290 visitors, how much money did they collect in entrance fees? **$1,450.00**

4. A local environmental group is planning to hike up Enchanted Rock. The group will cover each member's entrance fee and will provide lunch for its members. The group budgets $75.00 for lunch, regardless of the number of people on the hike. Complete the table to show the total expenses of the group based on the number of people on the hike.

Input, x	5	10	15	20	25	30
Output, y	$100.00	$125.00	$150.00	$175.00	$200.00	$225.00

5. Write an equation to represent the function displayed in the table.
y = 5x + 75

6. The group will hike up the dome at a rate of 1500 feet per hour. What is their hiking speed per minute? **25 feet per minute**

7. Complete the table to show the progression of their hike.

Input (min), x	1	3	5	8	10	12	15	17
Output (feet), y	25	75	125	200	250	300	375	425

8. Write an equation that represents the function displayed in the table.
y = 25x

9. At the rate given, how long will it take the group to reach the top of Enchanted Rock? **17 minutes**

Chapter 6 Assessment Answer Key

Quiz 1 (Lessons 6-1 and 6-2)
Page 53

1. $\frac{4}{7}$; for every 4 cats there are 7 dogs

2. $\frac{2}{1}$; for every 2 dimes there is 1 quarter

3. $\frac{4}{5}$

4. $21

5. $1.50

Quiz 2 (Lessons 6-3 and 6-4)
Page 53

1. No; the unit rates are not the same.

2. Yes; since the unit rates are the same, $\frac{\$5}{1\ hr}$, the rates are proportional.

3. 25

4. 4

5. 50

Quiz 3 (Lessons 6-5 and 6-6)
Page 54

1. multiply the position number by 3; $3n$; 36

2. subtract 5 from the position number; $n - 5$; 7

3. multiply the position number by 7; $7n$; 84

4. D

5. Subtract 6; 48

Quiz 4 (Lesson 6-7)
Page 54

1. $y = 4x$

2. $y = 12x$

3.

Touchdowns	1	2	3
Points	6	12	18

4. $p = 6t$

5. 42

Mid-Chapter Test
Page 55

1. B

2. H

3. D

4. G

5. C

6. No; the unit rates are not the same.

7. No; the unit rates are not the same.

8. Yes; since the unit rates are the same, $\frac{45\ points}{1\ game}$, the rates are proportional.

9. 10

10. 9

Answers

Chapter 6 Assessment Answer Key

Vocabulary Test
Page 56

Form 1
Page 57

Page 58

1. _____equation_____

2. _____term_____

3. ___Equivalent___

4. ____sequence____

5. ____constant____

6. _____adding_____

7. ____unit rate____

8. _____scaling_____

9. ____the same____

Sample answer: a comparison of two amounts by division
10. _____division_____

1. __D__

2. __F__

3. __B__

4. __H__

5. __B__

6. __F__

7. __C__

8. __J__

9. __B__

10. __F__

11. __C__

12. __J__

13. __B__

14. __F__

Yes; the unit rates
$\dfrac{10\ ft}{1\ in.}$ **are equivalent,**
B: $\dfrac{200\ ft}{20\ in.} = \dfrac{350\ ft}{35\ in.}$

Chapter 6 Assessment Answer Key

Form 2A
Page 59

1. __D__

2. __G__

3. __B__

4. __H__

5. __C__

6. __G__

7. __A__

8. __H__

Page 60

9. __B__

10. __H__

11. __D__

12. __F__

13. __C__

14. __F__

B: __No; the unit rates are not the same.__

Copyright © Glencoe/McGraw-Hill, a division of The McGraw-Hill Companies, Inc.

Form 2B
Page 61

1. __D__

2. __G__

3. __B__

4. __F__

5. __B__

6. __J__

7. __A__

8. __F__

Answers

(continued on the next page)

Chapter 6 Assessment Answer Key

Form 2B *(continued)*
Page 62

Form 2C
Page 63

Page 64

9. __C__

10. __F__

11. __B__

12. __G__

13. __B__

14. __H__

B: Yes; the unit rates
$\frac{5 \text{ baseball cards}}{9 \text{ football cards}}$ are
equivalent,
$\frac{10 \text{ baseball cards}}{18 \text{ football cards}} = \frac{15 \text{ baseball cards}}{27 \text{ football cards}}$

1. $\dfrac{8}{25}$

2. $\dfrac{9}{2}$

3. $\dfrac{53 \text{ km}}{1 \text{ h}}$

4. $\dfrac{\$5}{1 \text{ month}}$

5. __30__

6. No; the unit rates are not the same.

7. Yes; the unit rates are the same $\dfrac{3 \text{ hr}}{\$18} = \dfrac{5 \text{ hr}}{\$30}$.

8. __30__

9. __10__

10. __2__

11. __26__

12.

13. multiply by 8

14. __8n__

15. __120__

16. $y = 3x$

17. $y = 9x$

18. $y = 12x$

B: __96 breaths__

Chapter 6 Assessment Answer Key

Form 2D
Page 65

1. $\dfrac{1}{20}$

2. $\dfrac{3}{5}$

3. $\dfrac{30 \text{ miles}}{1 \text{ gal}}$

4. $\dfrac{30 \text{ students}}{1 \text{ class}}$

5. 9

6. Yes; the unit rates $\dfrac{5 \text{ calories}}{1 \text{ min}}$ are the same; $\dfrac{100 \text{ calories}}{20 \text{ min}} = \dfrac{175 \text{ calories}}{35 \text{ min}}$.

7. No; the unit rates are not the same.

8. 10

9. 7

10. 8

Page 66

11. 85

12.
```
•  •  •  •
•  •  •  •
•  •  •  •
•  •  •  •
```

13. subtract 6

14. $n - 6$

15. 10

16. $y = 4x$

17. $y = 8x$

18. $y = 11x$

B: 108 breaths

Answers

Chapter 6 Assessment Answer Key

Form 3
Page 67

1. $\dfrac{3}{22}$

2. $\dfrac{7}{11}$

3. $\dfrac{2.7 \text{ heartbeats}}{1 \text{ s}}$

4. $\dfrac{22.5 \text{ push-ups}}{1 \text{ min}}$

5. $16

6. 6

7. No; the unit rates are not the same.

8. Yes; the unit rates are the same $\dfrac{\$7}{\text{car}} = \dfrac{\$168}{24 \text{ cars}} = \dfrac{\$280}{40 \text{ cars}}$.

9. 4

10. 40

11. 16

Page 68

12. 24

13. 2005; $26,000

14. multiply by 9

15. $9n$

16. 144

17. $63

18. $y = 5x$

19. $y = 7x$

20. $y = 14x$

B: $2n + 3$

Chapter 6 Assessment Answer Key

Page 69, Extended-Response Test
Scoring Rubric

Level	Specific Criteria
4	The student demonstrates a **thorough understanding** of the mathematics concepts and/or procedures embodied in the task. The student has responded correctly to the task, used mathematically sound procedures, and provided clear and complete explanations and interpretations. The response may contain minor flaws that do not detract from the demonstration of a thorough understanding.
3	The student demonstrates an **understanding** of the mathematics concepts and/or procedures embodied in the task. The student's response to the task is essentially correct with the mathematical procedures used and the explanations and interpretations provided demonstrating an essential but less than thorough understanding. The response may contain minor errors that reflect inattentive execution of the mathematical procedures or indications of some misunderstanding of the underlying mathematics concepts and/or procedures.
2	The student has demonstrated only a **partial understanding** of the mathematics concepts and/or procedures embodied in the task. Although the student may have used the correct approach to obtaining a solution or may have provided a correct solution, the student's work lacks an essential understanding of the underlying mathematical concepts. The response contains errors related to misunderstanding important aspects of the task, misuse of mathematical procedures, or faulty interpretations of results.
1	The student has demonstrated a **very limited understanding** of the mathematics concepts and/or procedures embodied in the task. The student's response to the task is incomplete and exhibits many flaws. Although the student has addressed some of the conditions of the task, the student reached an inadequate conclusion and/or provided reasoning that was faulty or incomplete. The response exhibits many errors or may be incomplete.
0	The student has provided a **completely incorrect** solution or uninterpretable response, or no response at all.

Answers

Chapter 6 Assessment Answer Key

Page 69, Extended-Response Test
Sample Answers

In addition to the scoring rubric found on page A29, the following sample answers may be used as guidance in evaluating open-ended assessment items.

1. **a.** A ratio is the comparison of two numbers by division.

   b. 3 out of 4, 3:4, 3 to 4, $\frac{3}{4}$

   c. A rate is a ratio that compares two different units of measure. A unit rate is a rate that is in the per unit form. A unit rate is written with a denominator of 1. An example of a unit rate is 50 miles in 1 hour or 50 miles per hour. An example of rate that is not a unit rate is 50 miles in 2 hours.

   d. A proportion is a statement that two ratios are equivalent.

   e. Sample answer: If two out of five students in Mrs. Junkin's class have a dog, predict how many of the 200 students in the school have a dog.

   f. $\frac{2}{5} = \frac{x}{200}$

   $$\overset{\times 40}{\underset{\times 40}{\frac{2}{5} = \frac{80}{200}}}$$

   Since 5 × 40 = 200, multiply the numerator and denominator by 40.

   So, about 80 students out of the 200 students can be expected to have a dog.

2. **a.** Multiply the number of tickets purchased by 7 to find the total cost.

   b. $7x$, where x is the number of tickets purchased.

   c. $y = 7x$; $y =$ the total cost and $x =$ the number of tickets purchased.

   d. $y = 7x$
   $y = 7 \times 7$
   $y = \$49$
   It will cost a family $49 to buy 7 tickets.

   e. $y = 7x$
   $420 = 7x$
   THINK: $7 \times 60 = 420$
   So, the sixth grade class bought 60 tickets.

Chapter 6 Assessment Answer Key

Standardized Test Practice

Page 70   Page 71

1. Ⓐ Ⓑ ● Ⓓ   10. Ⓕ Ⓖ ● Ⓙ

2. Ⓕ ● Ⓗ Ⓙ   11. Ⓐ Ⓑ Ⓒ ●

3. Ⓐ Ⓑ Ⓒ ●

                             12. ● Ⓖ Ⓗ Ⓙ

4. Ⓕ Ⓖ ● Ⓙ   13. Ⓐ Ⓑ ● Ⓓ

5. Ⓐ Ⓑ ● Ⓓ

                             14. ● Ⓖ Ⓗ Ⓙ

6. Ⓕ Ⓖ Ⓗ ●

                             15. ___209.91___

7. Ⓐ Ⓑ ● Ⓓ

                             16. ___25___

8. Ⓕ Ⓖ Ⓗ ●

9. Ⓐ Ⓑ ● Ⓓ

(continued on the next page)

Answers

Chapter 6 Assessment Answer Key

17. $2 \times 3 \times 11$

18.

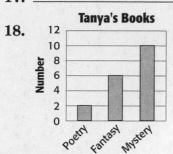

19. $1.375, 1.44, 1.5,$ $2.5, 8.4$

20. $\dfrac{\$0.25}{1 \text{ bottle}}$

21. Yes; the unit rates

$\dfrac{3 \text{ mi}}{16 \text{ min}}$ are equivalent

$\dfrac{15 \text{ mi}}{80 \text{ min}} = \dfrac{60 \text{ mi}}{320 \text{ min}}.$

22a. subtract 4 from the position number

22b. $n - 4$

22c. 12

22d. $v = n - 4$